Eat Out, Eat Right!

A guide to healthier restaurant eating

Hope S. Warshaw, M.M.Sc., R.D.

COMPLIMENTS OF

enteric-coated

Ecotrin®

THE MIRACLE OF ASPIRIN MADE SAFER™

Surrey Books

CHICAGO

EAT OUT, EAT RIGHT is published by Surrey Books, Inc.,
230 E. Ohio St., Suite 120, Chicago, Illinois 60611.

This book is manufactured in the U.S.A.

Library of Congress Cataloging-in-Publication data:
Warshaw, Hope S., 1954–
    Eat out, eat right / Hope S. Warshaw.
    152 p.   cm.
    ISBN 0-940625-45-8 : $5.95
    1. Nutrition.   2. Restaurants, lunch rooms, etc.—United States.
I. Title.
RA784.W364   1993
613.2—dc20   92-19081
                                                            CIP

Editorial and production: *Bookcrafters, Inc., Chicago*
Cover design and art direction: *Hughes & Co., Chicago*
Illustrations: *Elizabeth Allen*

For quantity purchases and prices, contact Surrey Books at the address
above.

CONTENTS

Foreword by Dr. Craig T. January   **1**

1. The Art of Healthier Eating Out   **3**

2. Mexican Style   **15**

3. Italian Style   **24**

4. Pizza Style   **33**

5. Chinese Style   **37**

6. Thai Style   **48**

7. Japanese Style   **59**

8. Indian Style   **68**

9. Middle Eastern Style   **78**

10. French/Continental Style   **87**

11. Seafood Style   **97**

12. American Style   **105**

13. Fast-Food Style   **114**

14. Luncheon Style   **124**

15. Salad Bar Style   **131**

16. Breakfast and Brunch   **136**

17. Airline Style   **144**

18. Beverages   **148**

To . . .

my wonderful expanded family; supportive professional buddies; fabulous personal friends; and clients from whom I have learned more than textbooks ever taught.

Acknowledgments:

A big thanks to Surrey Books: Susan Schwartz, publisher, who recognized the need for this book; Dana Metes, publicist; Gene DeRoin, editor; and Sally Hughes, artist.

Foreword

No one is born with coronary heart disease. Rather, it and heart attack are acquired illnesses. Sadly, they are acquired by far too many Americans as a result of choosing unhealthy lifestyle options such as smoking, shunning exercise, and eating a diet of high-fat, high-cholesterol foods.

Diet is central to good health in general, and it is even more critical to heart health. Thus, it is essential to establish healthy eating patterns in the interest of staying well and reducing the risk of heart attack and stroke. That means reducing fat, especially saturated fat, and cholesterol in favor of foods high in fiber and carbohydrates as well as minimizing sweets, sugar, and sodium.

For most of us, embarking on a healthful new eating program is not easy. It implies changes in grocery shopping and food preparation, and it means learning to enjoy different tastes in smaller quantities. Hard enough to accomplish in your own home— but what happens when you eat out?

How can we maintain a healthful low-fat, low-cholesterol diet in a restaurant when confronted with a menu burgeoning with Mexican treats or Chinese delicacies or Continental creations? How can one pick the foods that are rich in fiber and carbohydrates—and make sure their benefits are not destroyed by fat-laden cooking techniques? How does one cope with that tempting downtown salad bar at lunchtime or the fast-food offerings when you take the kids for burgers? This book has the answers.

In the pages that follow, Hope Warshaw, a distinguished dietitian, shows us how to enjoy a wide range of foods and tastes in over a dozen kinds of restaurants—without violating the tenets of healthful eating. Indeed, she makes it clear that a healthy diet does not mean saddling yourself with a bland, unappetizing array of tasteless foods. As you will see, choosing wisely in restaurants can lead not only to good health but to dining pleasure as well.

In my own cardiology practice, I have faced repeatedly the reality that most people still do not eat healthfully, even patients who have already had a heart attack or heart surgery. Perhaps they do not clearly understand the negative effects of poor diet. Perhaps they do not know that the Framingham Heart Study, begun in 1948, has never reported a heart attack in anyone with total cholesterol under 150 mg/dL! But it's not the restaurant's responsibility to educate its clientele. Each individual must take control of his or her eating patterns after deciding that a healthy diet—both at home and in restaurants—is worth the effort.

Choosing healthful items from a restaurant menu is not among the most difficult of life's decisions. But you must be willing to give up permanently high-fat nutritional disasters in favor of healthier—and usually just as tasty—choices. This book contains the fundamental information you need to make informed selections when eating in restaurants. Use it in good health.

Craig T. January, M.D., Ph.D.
Associate Professor of Medicine, University of Chicago

The art of
Healthier Eating Out

Whether you're lavishing three hours over a very expensive meal in a French cafe or simply rushing through one of the many fast-food franchises for lunch on the run, the principles of healthy eating out remain the same. In fact, the basic tenets for healthy restaurant eating, albeit with a few extra precautions and recommendations, are the same as for healthful eating at home.

BASIC RULES OF THE ROAD

There are six *Rules of the Road* for healthier dining out. These watchwords will guide you in virtually any restaurant. The six Rules of the Road will be

revisited time and time again in the pages ahead.
They are easy to master:

1. Keep track of eating-out frequency
2. Choose restaurants with care
3. Make savvy menu choices
4. Hold the line on fat
5. Order food "as you like it"
6. Practice portion control

1. Keep Track of Eating-Out Frequency

Let's face it: it's more difficult to stay on track when
eating out than when eating at home. You do not have
as much control over the salt, butter, oil, etc., as in
your own kitchen. Beyond that, restaurants offer
taste treats, not available at home, that whet your
appetite. For these reasons, it is important to monitor how often you eat out.

Here's the key to success: the more frequently
you eat out, the more closely choices and portions
should be checked. For many people, it is common to
eat lunch out five days and dinner out one or two
times a week. If caution is cast to the wind on most
occasions, the waistline will likely bulge, and there
may be health consequences in years ahead. However, if you dine out on the average of twice a week,
you can take a bit more liberty in your food choices.

Another factor to consider are your specific
nutrition goals. If simply eating healthier by cutting
down on fats, cholesterol, and salt is the goal and you
eat out infrequently, you've got a bit more liberty. But
if you must monitor saturated fat, cholesterol,
sodium, or other nutrients due to a health concern, it
will be important to control food choices more
strictly. So be clear about health and nutrition goals,
and establish a frequency of eating out that fits your
lifestyle.

2. Choose Restaurants with Care

The first order of business is to choose restaurants that serve what you want. Be careful not to find yourself reading a limited menu with minimal choices. Choosing an appropriate restaurant might require assertiveness if you are with a group of people. Let your needs be known.

In many instances you'll be familiar with the menu from previous excursions. Or maybe you have heard about the restaurant from friends or through advertising. In the rare instance when you are completely unfamiliar with the menu, ask questions about healthier options, types of food preparation, and the chef's willingness to grant special requests. Call ahead to assure your comfort level.

3. Make Savvy Menu Choices

The biggest challenge is to make menu selections that are both satisfying to your taste buds and healthy. Most menus represent a cross-section from nutritious delights to nutritional disasters. The challenge of making appropriate decisions can be especially difficult when hunger is getting the best of you and your resistance to "danger" foods is faltering.

When making menu choices, first decide on the main focus. Will you choose an entree? If so, what comes with it? Do you want a salad or soup in addition, or will the entree be enough? Maybe you have decided on an appetizer instead of an entree and to splurge on a dessert; or will an appetizer and salad do the trick? In many eating situations, such as a fast-food meal, a simple lunch, or pizza and salad, the focus is clearer.

A few words of caution. Do not set yourself up for overeating and/or selecting poor choices by starving during the day to "save calories" for the restaurant meal. Also, avoid over-ordering, especially when hunger is rampant. Order with your stomach in mind—not your eyes. If you have been to the restaurant previously, do not tempt yourself with the menu. Plan your order prior to crossing the threshold. Do not even take hold of the menu.

4. Hold the Line on Fat

When trying to eat healthier, choosing menu items to minimize fat is a vital skill. Fat's prime rule is to enhance taste and flavor. It certainly does that, whether butter, margarine, cream, or bacon. However, while enhancing flavor, fat also adds lots of calories and next to no food volume.

Fat is the "devil" of restaurant menus. Consider a medium baked potato, at about 100 calories. Add 1 teaspoon of margarine and 2 tablespoons of sour cream. You have added another 100 calories with no more food volume. Beyond calories, fats may also contribute saturated fat and cholesterol—unwanted additions.

Fat creeps into restaurant selections in many ways. Consider appetizers that are often fried or contain high-fat ingredients. Think about Italian fried mozzarella sticks or Chinese fried jumbo shrimp. Entree choices such as duck or prime rib are high in fat even before other fat-laden ingredients are added. Fat is frequently added as butter, cream, sour cream, cheese, mayonnaise, or cooking oil. Entrees may be fried or sauteed, incorporating fat in the cooking process. Dessert is the final fat danger zone—think about ice cream, chocolate mousse, or cheesecake. At the table, bread and butter, cheese and crackers, or nacho chips greet you. Once the meal is served, more fat is often added in the form of salad dressing, buttered vegetables, sour cream for potatoes, and cream for coffee or tea.

Fat is the most saturated form of calories. Volume being equal, carbohydrate and protein foods have about half the calories of fat. For this reason, it is essential that you become a good fat detective. Find ways to pay careful attention to how fat creeps into restaurant foods.

5. Order Food "As You Like It"

Special requests are often necessary to have food "as you like it." If your special requests are reasonable and asked for in a friendly yet assertive manner, you usually will have your wishes granted. Here are several hints to keep in mind to bolster your confidence. First, remember that you are paying the bill. You have the privilege to have food prepared the way you desire. You may request that the chef leave something off or reduce the quantity of a particular item. Second, most businesses want and need your patronage. It is probable that if your special requests are courteously granted and you are pleased with the results, you will return and—better yet—refer friends and family. Third, waitpersons are getting used to special requests because more people are carefully watching the foods they consume.

Special requests encompass asking for a substitution or having an item served on the side, such as salad dressing, a sauce, or gravy. Having a high-fat or high-sodium item served on the side allows you to control your intake. You might request that an item be broiled dry rather than drenched in butter, or that a Chinese stir-fry dish be cooked using less oil or soy sauce. A special request might mean that an item be left off, such as potato chips or potato salad, or that a substitution of baked potato be made for French fries.

As special requests are made more frequently, you will realize that you are not ruffling any feathers. When you initiate this practice, think of using phrases such as: "Do you think the chef would be able to . . . ," "I'd really appreciate it if you would . . . ," or "Can I get . . . on the side?"

6. Practice Portion Control

Once you have placed your order, the next step in healthy restaurant eating is to practice the art of portion control. Unfortunately, you are usually served more food than you need. It is easy to rationalize eating more and continuing your membership in the clean plate club. It is especially easy to eat more of the foods that are "good for you"—fish, fruits, or vegetables—under the assumption that it's never too much.

Practicing and mastering portion control is not easy, but practice can make perfect. Several strategies are helpful. Begin by purposely leaving a few bites on the plate. Most restaurants have "doggie bags" and are more than happy to wrap extras. "Doggie bags" are more acceptable as people become more conscious of limiting quantities. Here's a new twist: ask for a "doggie bag" when your meal is served, and immediately separate the restaurant portion from what you will take home. The theory "out of sight, out of mind . . . or mouth" is quite helpful. Sometimes "doggie bags" are unavailable or the situation does not lend itself to this request, perhaps at a business luncheon. If that is the case, portion out what you should eat and separate it from the rest. Place the "extra" food on a bread or salad plate. Graciously offer a taste to your dining companions—or just move it to the side.

Sharing is another portion-control strategy. You will need one or more willing dining partners. Try sharing an appetizer, salad, and entree and then have enough room to split a dessert. In some cuisines it is routine for people to share entrees—Chinese, Thai, Japanese, or when eating pizza. When sharing, be sure to make your food needs and desires known to your eating partners.

Another strategy is to signal the waitperson when you are done to remove your plate from the table. That will assist you in not overeating simply because the food is still in front of you.

When practicing the above skills, it is difficult to forget the childhood message about the Clean Plate Club. Granted, no one is encouraging the waste of food, but it is important to ask yourself whether it is better for your health if the food is eaten or left on the plate. Keep the following question in mind: is it better for the food to go to waste or to *your* waist?

TRICKS OF THE TRADE

There are many strategies and tactics, which I call *Tricks of the Trade*, to help you change current behaviors and attitudes. The following are among the most important:

1. Think "I Can-Do"
2. Stay a Step Ahead by Preplanning
3. Rethink Old Habits
4. Shrink the Gut
5. Enjoy More Than the Food

Over time, these Tricks of the Trade will become old hat, and eating healthier will become second nature.

1. Think "I Can-Do"

Dangerous preconceived notions and negative mind-sets about dining out easily and often lead to poor choices and overeating. It is important to recognize your lethal notions and slowly trade them in for a healthier and positive mindset. A common notion is that eating out is a special occasion, even though you do it two or three times a week. "Special occasion" translates into choosing whatever your taste buds desire and eating until you are stuffed.

Another detrimental behavior is to practice extreme caution when eating at home, yet casting all caution to the wind and "pigging out" in restaurants. Food is often used as a reward. Treating yourself "well" or rewarding yourself becomes synonymous with eating what you want—you had a rough day so you deserve fried appetizers or a decadent chocolate dessert. Food is also used to celebrate—a child's birthday, a friend's promotion—and, again, one may see an opportunity to "pig out."

Another set of notions connected with eating out involves "getting your money's worth." The attitude of "I'm paying for it so I might as well eat it" is a dangerous mindset. It only leads to overeating. This pitfall is one of many reasons to avoid "all you can eat" buffets.

After you have honestly owned up to your present attitudes, you are ready to establish new ones. First, it is important to believe that eating healthy is a priority to you. Second, you must believe that you will continue to enjoy dining out while ordering healthier foods. Enjoyment is key; no one continues to practice behaviors that are perceived as unpleasant.

2. Stay a Step Ahead by Preplanning

"Calorie banking" is a preplanning concept. Calorie banking teaches you to think ahead about what you are eating and will be eating. For example, if you know that you will be celebrating an occasion at a fancy restaurant, think about "banking" some calories for that meal through the day, or even start the day before. Over the course of a week, some occasions may be planned for more calories, perhaps on weekends or for social events. Conversely, some days can be low-calorie days—when you save calories to put in the "bank" for future use.

Another strategy for calorie account balancing is to add more exercise. Increasing the calories burned means putting more calories back in the bank. If your bank account is "balanced" at the end of the week, your weight should stay even. If you are overdrawn, you know the results. Sorry, there is no overdraft protection at this bank.

This same "banking" concept can be applied if you are watching your intake of cholesterol, sodium, saturated fat, or other nutrition components. For instance, if you are going out for high-sodium Chinese or Japanese food, make an effort to choose low-sodium foods during the day. Then, at the restaurant you have a bit more leeway, yet in the end your sodium bank account remains balanced.

Another helpful preplanning strategy is to have an order in mind prior to crossing the restaurant's threshold. You will likely visit restaurants you frequent and will have a good sense of the menu. For example, when you open most Chinese restaurant menus, you find listings of hot-and-sour soup, steamed white rice, chicken and broccoli, shrimp with assorted vegetables, and many other dishes. If you plan your order in advance, you are less tempted by smells, wandering eyes, and mouth-watering menu descriptions.

Another strategy for most-frequented dining spots is simply not to take a menu. This avoids taste bud fantasies and self-torture, with "should I" or "shouldn't I" questions. Have your mind made up prior to arriving. Another helpful tactic is be the first to order to make sure you will go through with your plan.

When you are deciding on menu choices, think about using soups and salads as fillers. This is helpful if you have arrived famished. A cup of brothy soup or a crunchy green salad might take the edge off your appetite. This strategy may help you fill up on healthier foods and be more successful in avoiding excesses. This tactic is especially useful if your dining companions are ordering high-fat appetizers.

3. Rethink Old Habits

Once you receive your food, several tricks are at your service. Eat slowly and savor the food. People generally eat too fast and barely give taste buds a chance to notice what is passing by. Keep in mind that it takes approximately 20 minutes for your stomach to notify your brain that you are full. So if you eat fast and finish a meal in 10 minutes, you have 10 more minutes left before your brain knows you have eaten. Look around the table for a dining partner eating at a snail's pace, and slow down with him or her.

You can slow the pace of eating by putting down utensils frequently. Take a few bites, place the knife and fork by the side of your plate, and enjoy the taste sensations. Try stopping for frequent sips of a beverage. This achieves two goals: it slows the pace of eating and fills you up with extra fluids.

4. Shrink the Gut

Knowing when enough is enough is vital. Unfortunately, most people respond to external rather than internal cues. For example, the external cue of a few more bites left on the plate encourages you to clean the plate. If you define fullness as that post-Thanksgiving-dinner-stuffed-turkey feeling or a clean plate, you are likely overeating frequently. If your reference point for fullness is leading you to overeat, it is time to shrink the gut.

The first challenge is to listen to your internal signals. How does your stomach feel when you have had enough to eat? This sensation is a message to put down your knife and fork rather than waiting for the old stuffed feeling to set in. The second challenge is to slow the pace of eating. This gives your body more time to recognize fullness. Third, take time to think about and enjoy what you are eating. These strategies can help increase your feeling of satiety, which makes portion control easier.

5. Enjoy More Than the Food

Frequently, in a restaurant you are so focused on the food due to time constraints, hunger, or other stresses that you do not enjoy the environment. If you train yourself to enjoy all aspects of the eating experience, limiting portions will be easier. Obviously, this strategy is not workable when cruising by the drive-in window of a fast-food chain to pick up lunch, which you guzzle down in 10 minutes. Nevertheless, it is extremely important to provide yourself a few minutes of relaxation at mealtimes, even if you are in a hurry and the main goal of eating is to refuel.

When you are dining out, take in the non-food niceties. Let yourself savor a few minutes of relaxation, concentrate on the conversation, look around and enjoy the ambiance, observe the people in your midst. Enjoy being waited on. Think about not having to cook, put away leftovers, clear the table, or wash the dishes. Simply put, look *beyond the food*.

HOW TO USE THIS BOOK

Eat Out, Eat Right presents a very simple and realistic "hands-on" approach to wise and healthy food choices within a wide range of restaurant cuisines. Each chapter familiarizes you with the positive nutrition traits as well as the pitfalls of a particular style of cooking. The "hands-on" advice in nearly every chapter includes:

Green Flag Words—The "go-ahead-and-order" signals.

Red Flag Words—The "stop-and-consider" words.

Special Requests—Phrases to use for healthful modifications of restaurant dishes.

The Menu—A generic menu for each cuisine, which identifies preferred choices.

May I Take Your Order—Two sample meals, one with lower calorie count and one with moderate, are given in most chapters. These meals are designed to fit into daily food plans that are based on healthy eating goals, with around 50% of calories from carbohydrate, 20% from protein, and 30% from fat; no more than 300 milligrams of cholesterol, and no more than 3,000 milligrams of sodium.

Low-Calorie Sample Meals: These meals contain 400–700 calories, with 30–35% of the calories derived from fat. The cholesterol count is about 100–200 milligrams per meal. Low-Calorie Sample Meals are based on a daily calorie consumption of 1,200–1,600 calories.

Moderate-Calorie Sample Meals: These meals contain approximately 600–1,000 calories, with 30–35% of the calories coming from fat. Cholesterol count is about 100–200 milligrams per meal. Moderate-Calorie Sample Meals are based on a daily intake of 1,800–2,200 calories.

"Guestimated" Exchanges: Exchange values are provided for each sample meal. These are based on the 1986 Exchange Lists for Meal Planning developed by The American Diabetes Association and The American Dietetic Association.

Nutrition Summary: Each sample meal is followed by a nutrition summary that "guestimates" the meal's nutrient composition. This information is based on sample recipes, nutrient composition tables from the United States Department of Agriculture (USDA), and information from restaurant companies. It is important to keep in mind that these are simply estimates.

Menu Lingo—Menus in ethnic restaurants often have tongue-twisting ingredients and preparation styles or menu items to decipher. This glossary of menu terms will help you understand the cuisines and make healthier choices.

Healthy Daily Eating Goals
30% Calories as fat
20% Calories as protein
50% Calories as carbohydrate
300 mg/day Cholesterol
3000 mg/day Sodium

Healthier eating out
Mexican Style

If you like foods moderately hot, spicy, and loaded with jalapeño peppers, Mexican food is probably high on your list of ethnic favorites. However, you might have second thoughts about the healthiness of Mexican cuisine. Memories of Mexican meals may conjure up thoughts of high-fat nacho chips topped with high-fat guacamole and sour cream or fried taco shells sprinkled with high-cholesterol shredded cheese. Fortunately, many Mexican meals can be quite healthy. Think of soft tacos filled with refried beans, lettuce, tomato, onions, and salsa; chicken enchiladas; or a Mexican salad. They are just a few of the great, healthier Mexican choices available.

THE MENU PROFILE

Successful and healthy dining on Mexican food takes some careful navigating around the menu. The three mainstay healthy ingredients—corn, beans, and chilies—find their way into most Mexican meals. On their own, they are nutritionally sound, but when incorporated into Mexican appetizers or entrees, they can result either in nutritional disasters or wise choices. Consider chilies, which go into chili con queso, a high-fat, spicy cheese dip, and also into salsa verde, a low-fat, hot green sauce. Corn or wheat is the main ingredient in tortillas. In a soft taco, the flour tortilla contains little fat, whereas taco shells are deep fried. So making the right choice is *numero uno.*

Another health benefit of Mexican food is the minimal focus on protein compared to a typical American meal. Compare the small quantity of meat, one to two ounces, in one enchilada to our familiar eight- to ten-ounce steak. This has its roots in the old practice of making a small amount of meat feed many mouths.

Fat is the villain in Mexican cuisine. Not only are there many fried items, but many Mexican recipes traditionally call for the use of lard or animal fat drippings. Both of these items contain cholesterol and saturated fat.

You might want to ask the waitperson to find out what type of fat is used in the cooking, especially if this is a restaurant you frequent. For instance, you might choose a soft enchilada rather than a taco if you know that the tortilla will be fried in lard. If vegetable oil is used for frying, you might feel better about ordering the chicken or beef fajitas. If calories are your biggest concern, then any preparation using fat should be limited.

Mexican food can also be high in sodium. Salt is used in many recipes, and a lot of food preparation is done in advance, such as preparing meats to stuff tacos or burritos. This makes it difficult to request holding the salt. However, if you are ordering a dish such as grilled chicken, fish, or beef in an upscale Mexican restaurant, you might be successful with a hold-the-salt request. Chips and salsa and large amounts of cheese can also contribute to raising the sodium level. Due to its zesty taste, small amounts of salsa can be used to add punch to salads or chicken and fish dishes. Green or red salsa is fine to use in small amounts.

Green Flag Words

- shredded spicy chicken
- spicy beef
- served with salsa (hot red tomato sauce)
- served with salsa verde (green chili sauce)
- covered with enchilada sauce
- topped with shredded lettuce, diced tomatoes, and onions
- served with or wrapped in a corn or flour tortilla
- grilled
- marinated
- picante sauce
- simmered
- mole sauce

Red Flag Words

- topped with sour cream
- served with guacamole
- topped, filled, covered with cheese
- shredded cheese
- served in fried tortilla shell
- stuffed with Mexican cheese
- chorizo (Mexican sausage) or bacon
- served over tortilla chips
- topped with black olives
- crispy
- fried or deep fried
- layered with refried beans

Special Requests
Mexican Style

- Please hold the sour cream.
- Please hold the guacamole.
- Please serve my salad without the fried tortilla shell (or nacho chips) but bring an order of soft tortillas on the side.
- Please remove (or don't bring) the chips and salsa from the table.
- Please hold the grated cheese.
- Would it be possible to get extra salsa on the side?
- Please put extra shredded lettuce, tomatoes, and chopped onions on the plate.
- May I substitute shredded spiced chicken for beef?
- Could I get this wrapped up to take home?

Typical Menu: Mexican Style

Appetizers

✓ **Tostada** chips with salsa
Tostada chips with guacamole
Nachos with melted cheese and jalapeño peppers
Chili con queso (melted cheese, green chilies, and peppers with corn tortilla chips)
✓ **Black bean soup,** cup or bowl
✓ **Chili con carne,** cup or bowl
✓ **Gazpacho** (spicy cold soup made from vegetables and tomatoes)

✓ indicates
preferred choices

Salads	✓ **Dinner salad** (mixed greens, cheese, and tomato, topped with onions)

✓ **Dinner salad** (mixed greens, cheese, and tomato, topped with onions)

✓ **Mexican salad** (lettuce, tomato, and red peppers, topped with two kinds of cheese, served in crisp tortilla shell, with creamy garlic dressing)

Taco salad (choice of spicy ground meat or shredded chicken, topped with refried beans, lettuce, tomatoes, and onions, topped with sour cream and guacamole and served in crisp tortilla shell)

Mexican Specialties

Chimichangas, beef or chicken (flour tortillas filled with spicy beef or chicken and Monterey Jack cheese, fried and topped with tomato sauce)

✓ **Fajitas** (marinated beef, chicken, or shrimp grilled with onions, green peppers, lettuce, diced tomatoes, sour cream, and guacamole)

✓ **Enchiladas** (corn tortillas stuffed with either ground beef or shredded chicken and topped with tomato sauce, shredded cheese and sour cream)

✓ **Tacos** (fried flour tortillas stuffed with choice of spicy ground beef, shredded chicken, or a seafood blend; loaded with shredded lettuce, diced tomatoes, and onions and topped with cheese)

✔ **Burritos** (large flour tortilla
filled with choice of refried beans
and cheese, spicy ground beef, or
chicken; served with tomato
sauce and topped with shredded
cheese)

Mexican Dinners   Served with refried beans and
Mexican rice
Flautas con crema (crisp rolled
tortillas stuffed with shredded
chicken or beef, topped with a
spicy cream sauce)
✔ **Chili verde** (pork simmered with
green chilies, vegetables, and
Mexican spices)
Mole pollo (boned chicken breast
cooked in mole sauce, hot and
spicy)
✔ **Camarones de hacha** (fresh
shrimp sauteed in a red and green
tomato coriander sauce)
Carne asada (grilled sirloin steak
served in an enchilada sauce with
chorizo and guacamole)
✔ **Arroz con pollo** (boneless
chicken breast served on top of
spicy rice with vegetable sauce)

Side Orders   ✔ **Mexican rice**
Refried beans
✔ **Black beans**
✔ **Tortillas,** flour or corn
✔ **Salsa**
Guacamole

Desserts	✓ **Flan** (caramel-flavored custard) **Sopaipillas** (deep-fried dough, tossed in sugar)

May I Take Your Order

Low-Calorie Sample Meal	**Chili con carne** *Quantity:* 1 cup *Exchanges:* 1 starch; 1 meat; 1 fat **Dinner salad** (hold the cheese and dressing) *Quantity:* 2 cups *Exchanges:* 2 vegetable **Salsa** for dressing *Exchanges:* free **Chicken taco,** soft *Quantity:* 1 *Exchanges:* 1 starch; 2 meat; 1 fat
Nutrition Summary	480 calories 35% calories as fat 26% calories as protein 39% calories as carbohydrate 67 mg cholesterol 1600 mg sodium
Moderate-Calorie Sample Meal	**Black bean soup** *Quantity:* 1 cup *Exchanges:* 2 starches **Chili verde** served with 2 flour tortillas *Quantity:* 1½ cups *Exchanges:* 2 starch; 3 meat; 2 fat; 2 vegetable **Mexican rice** *Quantity:* ⅓ cup *Exchanges:* 1 starch

Refried beans
Quantity: ⅓ cup
Exchanges: 1 starch; 1 fat
Mexican beer
Quantity: 12 oz.

Nutrition Summary		
	992	calories
	27%	calories as fat
	17%	calories as protein
	48%	calories as carbohydrate
	8%	calories as alcohol
	96	mg cholesterol
	2100	mg sodium

Mexican Menu Lingo

Arroz—Spanish word for rice. Mexican rice is made from long-grain white rice with sauteed tomatoes, onions, and garlic added for flavor.

Burrito—a wheat flour tortilla (soft, not fried) filled with either chicken, beef, or cheese in addition to refried beans; served rolled up and covered with a light tomato-based enchilada sauce.

Carne—Spanish word for meat.

Cerveza—Spanish word for beer.

Ceviche—raw fish, soaked or "cooked" in lime or lemon juice for many hours and served as an appetizer or light meal; the seafood used is often scallops.

Chili—there are over 100 different types of chilies native to Mexico. They are of different shapes, sizes, and colors, and they vary in level of spiciness from mild to hot, hotter, and hottest. Chilies are available fresh and dried.

Chili con carne—usually simply called "chili" in America, a thick soup made with tomatoes, onions, peppers, pinto beans, and ground or shredded beef; often served with raw chopped onions and shredded cheese.

Chimichanga—flour tortilla filled with beef, chicken, cheese, and/or beans; deep fried and served topped with tomato-based sauce.

Chorizo—Mexican pork sausage, hot and highly seasoned.

Cilantro—leafy green herb with a strong flavor frequently used in Mexican cooking; also called coriander.

Enchiladas—corn tortillas dipped in enchilada sauce, lightly fried, and then filled with a choice of chicken, beef, or cheese and served topped with light tomato-based enchilada sauce.

Fajitas—sauteed chicken or beef served with sauteed onions and green peppers, shredded lettuce, tomatoes, and guacamole; served with flour tortillas. Usually you roll your own at the table.

Flan—baked custard with a caramel top; contains mainly sugar, eggs, and cream, whole or condensed milk.

Gazpacho—spicy, cold tomato-based soup that contains pureed or pieces of raw vegetables.

Guacamole—mashed avocado, onion, tomatoes, garlic, lemon juice, and spices; served as a topping, as a dip with chips, or on the side. Avocado is high in fat; approximately 80 calories per 1/4 avocado, though the fat is mainly monounsaturated and contains no cholesterol.

Jalapeño chili—a type of chili often mistakenly referred to as a pepper. A very small, hot, green chili used to spice or top certain menu items.

Mole—refers to a "concoction," usually a spicy brown seasoning mixture for chicken or meats that contains a small amount of chocolate.

Quesadillas—flour tortillas filled with cheese and chili mixture; tortilla is rolled and then fried.

Refried beans—pinto beans that have been cooked and then refried in lard and seasoned with onions, garlic, and chili.

Salsa—hot red sauce made from tomatoes, onions, and chili; appears automatically on the table of most Mexican restaurants.

Salsa verde—very hot green sauce made from tomatillo, the Mexican green tomato, and other spices.

Taco—corn tortilla filled with meat or chicken, shredded cheese, lettuce, and tomatoes; usually the corn tortilla is fried in the shape of a "U." Soft taco is usually made with a flour tortilla and is not fried.

Tamale—spicy filling of either meat or chicken, surrounded by moist corn meal dough and wrapped in corn husks or banana leaves; they are then steamed.

Tortilla—the "bread" of Mexico, a very thin circle of dough made either from corn or flour; often corn tortillas are fried into taco shells or chips and served with salsa.

Tostadas—crisp, deep-fried tortilla chips, or the whole fried tortilla, which then may be covered with various toppings such as cheese, beans, lettuce, tomato, and/or onions.

3.

Healthier eating out
Italian Style

For many, Italian cuisine is on their bestseller list. Whether it be parmigiana, cacciatore, or scampi, there is a wonderful world of taste treats at Italian restaurants. And, better yet, many items are very healthy.

THE MENU PROFILE

Italian meals, eaten in a variety of Italian restaurants from inexpensive to costly, can range from healthy to nutritional disasters. Consider the following healthy Italian meal: a cup of minestrone or stracciatelle; linguine with white clam sauce; and, as enjoyed in Italy, a demitasse of espresso. At the opposite end of the spectrum, consider this high-fat, cholesterol, and sodium meal: several pieces of Italian garlic bread doused in olive oil; antipasto of various Italian cheeses, Genoa salami, marinated artichokes, and olives; an entree of fettucini Alfredo; and the well-known Italian dessert, cannoli. It is clear that you have a wide range of choices.

The portion-control strategy of sharing in an Italian restaurant can be quite helpful. If you have a willing dining companion, sharing allows you to taste and enjoy several items while minimizing the amounts you consume. Think about sharing straight through the meal. Start with an antipasto, such as mussels marinara, or split a salad, perhaps of marinated seafood. Think about sharing a pasta dish, or have one person order a pasta dish while the other orders a seafood or poultry dish. If you can afford the calories, split a dessert, maybe even four ways. After all, a taste is usually all you really want.

Green Flag Words

- lightly sauteed with onions
- shallots, peppers, mushrooms
- artichoke hearts
- sun-dried tomatoes
- spicy marinara sauce
- tomato-based sauce—marinara or cacciatore
- light red sauce
- red- or white-wine sauce
- light mushroom sauce
- capers, herbs, spices
- garlic and oregano, crushed tomatoes and spices
- florentine (spinach)
- grilled (often done to fish)
- red or white clam sauce
- primavera (make sure it is not a cream sauce)
- lemon sauce
- piccata

Red Flag Words

- Alfredo
- carbonara
- saltimbocca
- parmigiana
- pancetta
- oil
- stuffed with cheese
- prosciutto
- mozzarella cheese, pecorino cheese (Romano)
- creamy wine sauce
- creamy cheese or mushroom sauce
- egg and cheese batter
- veal sausage
- manicotti, cannelloni, lasagne, ravioli

Special Requests Italian Style

- Please don't put the bread down here.
- Please remove my plate; I'm finished now.
- I'll take the rest of this home in a doggie bag.
- Please hold the Parmesan (or grated) cheese, bacon, olives, pine nuts.
- Hold the sauce on the pasta.
- Please use only a small amount of sauce over the pasta.
- I'd like the appetizer-size pasta, and please bring it when you bring the other entrees.
- Would you ask the chef to avoid using any extra salt.

Typical Menu: Italian Style

| Antipasto | **Antipasto for Two** (marinated mushrooms, artichoke hearts, Genoa salami, and pecorino cheese)
Prosciutto wrapped around melon
✓ **Marinated calamari**
Garlic bread
✓ **Marinated mushrooms**
✓ **Clams** steamed in white wine
Fried mozzarella sticks with marinara sauce |
|---|---|
| Zuppa | ✓ **Tortellini in broth**
✓ **Pasta e fagioli** (bean and pasta soup)
✓ **Minestrone**
Lentil and sausage |
| Insalata | ✓ **Arugula and Belgian endive** with balsamic vinaigrette dressing
✓ **Insalata frutte di mare** (marinated seafood, scallops, shrimp, and calamari in a light marinade, served on a bed of greens)
✓ **Insalata di casa** (house salad with greens, tomato, and onion) |

✓ indicates
preferred choices

Caesar salad (greens with buttery croutons, Parmesan cheese, and creamy Caesar dressing)

Pasta

Cannelloni stuffed with ricotta cheese and spinach, topped with a light tomato sauce

✓ **Ziti Bolognese** (tubular noodles topped with a light tomato sauce of sauteed meat, celery, carrots, and onions)

Fettucini Alfredo (thin, flat pasta served with a creamy cheese sauce)

✓ **Angel hair pasta** with white clam sauce

✓ **Fusilli primavera** (a spiral, long pasta topped with a blend of spicy sauteed seasonal vegetables)

Carne*

Veal piccata (medallions of veal lightly sauteed in a butter, lemon, and wine sauce)

✓ **Veal cacciatore** (veal cutlet topped with tomato sauce and sauteed onions, mushrooms, and peppers)

✓ **Chicken primavera** (breast of chicken lightly sauteed and topped with sauteed seasonal vegetables)

Chicken parmigiana (chicken cutlet baked with mozzarella cheese and tomato sauce)

✓ **Chicken in wine sauce** (sauteed breast of chicken, roasted peppers, and mushrooms, with Burgundy wine, fresh garlic, and rosemary)

Pesce*

✓ **Shrimp primavera** (sauteed shrimp and garden vegetables served on bed of angel hair pasta)

✓ **Shrimp marinara** (shrimp lightly sauteed in garlic and topped with tomato sauce)

Scallops marsala (sauteed scallops in a mushroom and marsala wine sauce)

Shrimp scampi (shrimp sauteed in olive oil, fresh garlic, white wine, lemon, and oregano)

✓ **Sole primavera** (fillet of sole sauteed with an assortment of seasonal fresh vegetables, zucchini, peppers, and tomatoes)

*These items served with a bowl of spaghetti topped with your choice of marinara sauce or olive oil and garlic.

Dolce

Spumoni
Cannoli
✓ **Italian ice**
Tortoni

May I Take Your Order

Low-Calorie Sample Meal	**Arugula and Belgian endive salad** (request balsamic vinegar on the side) *Quantity:* 2 cups *Exchanges:* 2 vegetable **Fusilli primavera** (hold sauce and use that from entree) *Quantity:* 1 cup *Exchanges:* 2 starch **Shrimp primavera** (eat half) *Quantity:* 1½ cups *Exchanges:* 3–4 meat (lean); 2 fat; 2 vegetable **Espresso** *Quantity:* 1 cup *Exchanges:* free
Nutrition Summary	450 calories 21% calories as fat 34% calories as protein 45% calories as carbohydrate 160 mg cholesterol 650 mg sodium
Moderate-Calorie Sample Meal	**Tortellini in broth** *Quantity:* 1 cup *Exchanges:* 1 starch **Insalata di casa** (dressing on the side) *Quantity:* 1 cup *Exchanges:* 1 vegetable **Basil vinaigrette dressing** (on the side) *Quantity:* 1 tablespoon *Exchanges:* 1 fat

Veal cacciatore
Quantity: ½ portion (½ in doggie bag)
Exchanges: 3 meat; 1 vegetable; 1 fat
Spaghetti (hold sauce and use that from entree)
Quantity: 1½ cups
Exchanges: 3 starch

Nutrition Summary	
770	calories
31%	calories as fat
24%	calories as protein
45%	calories as carbohydrate
100 mg	cholesterol
1050 mg	sodium

Know Your Pastas

Pasta, meaning "paste" or "dough," is a staple in Italian restaurants. Pasta is basically created from flour (sometimes durum and sometimes all-purpose flour), water, and/or eggs. These ingredients are used to create a wide variety of different pastas, from angel hair to ziti.

Unlike Italy of yesterday, you see many differently colored and spiced pastas in American restaurants today. There are whole-wheat, tomato, spinach, artichoke, and many more types of pastas. Here is a basic primer to help you "Know Your Pastas" and have an easier time deciding which one to order.

Agnolotti—crescent-shaped pieces of pasta, stuffed with one ingredient or a combination of cheese, meat, and spinach.

Angel hair—the thinnest and finest of the "long" pasta family, it is quite light in consistency and often served with light sauces.

Cannelloni—large, tubular pasta, similar to manicotti, it is stuffed with one ingredient or a combination of cheese, meat, and spinach.

Capellitti—meaning a "little hat," these are small, stuffed pastas that look like little tortellini; often stuffed with cheese or meats.

Fettucini—flat, long noodle about ¼-inch wide (wider than linguine).

Fusilli—spiral-shaped long pasta, fusilli is round like spaghetti.

Gnocchi—little dumplings, in ½-inch pieces made from either flour, potato, or a combination of both; often topped with sauce.

Lasagne—the widest noodle among the long, flat pastas; found with either smooth or scalloped edges.

Linguine—flat, long noodle about ⅛-inch wide (thinner than fettucini).

Manicotti—long, tubular noodle about 2 inches in diameter, most often stuffed with cheese and/or meat and served with tomato sauce.

Mostaccioli—short, tubular noodle about 1½ inches long.

Penne—short, tubular noodle quite similar to mostaccioli and rigatoni.

Polenta—corn meal and water mixture, which is cooked, poured on a board to harden, and served with a sauce.

Ravioli—pasta about 2 inches square, with corrugated edges, always stuffed with cheese, spinach, or meats in combination or singly.

Rigatoni—short, tubular noodle quite similar to penne and mostaccioli.

Risotto—Italian short-grain rice that has a creamy consistency when cooked; often mixed with butter and cheese before serving.

Shells—noodles in the shape of conch shells, called *conchiglie* in Italian, and found in a variety of sizes; sometimes larger ones are stuffed, and most are served topped with tomato sauce.

Spaghetti—thin, round pasta (also called vermicelli); the most commonly known pasta in America.

Tortellini—small pastas, stuffed and joined at the ends to form a ring: a larger version of capellitti.

Ziti—a short, tubular pasta similar to mostaccioli.

Healthier eating out
Pizza Style

Yes, pizza is Italian, but we have given it a special chapter. After all, pizza is almost as American as apple pie. There probably isn't a town or city where you can't at least get a cheese and tomato pizza. Pizza is eaten for lunch, for dinner, and sometimes cold for breakfast or for a late-night snack.

THE PIZZA PROFILE

Think about it. What is pizza? The dough is basically flour, yeast, salt, and water—no fat, no cholesterol, few calories. Then a tomato sauce is added—another low-calorie item. Next, the cheese is spread, which, of course, is high in calories and fat. But how much cheese is really on one slice of pizza—¾ to 1 ounce? The final step is to add other toppings. Will they be low-calorie mushrooms, onions, spinach, and tomato slices, or will you order extra cheese, pepperoni, and sausage?

There seems to be a move afoot to be more creative with ingredients and the combinations of items used on pizza. That is great for the nutrition conscious because many of the new ingredients are vegetables and other lower-calorie foods (see Green Flag Pizza Toppings). The great spicy taste of pizza can be retained while reducing the fat, cholesterol, sodium, and calories contained in extra cheese, sausage, and pepperoni.

There are really many tasty, low-fat and low-calorie toppings with which to load your pizza. Choose among healthy ingredients such as spinach, mushrooms, broccoli, and roasted peppers, to name but a few.

Green Flag Toppings

- green and red peppers
- roasted peppers
- onions
- sliced tomatoes
- mushrooms
- black olives
- broccoli and eggplant
- garlic
- feta cheese
- spinach
- chicken
- shrimp or crabmeat
- artichoke hearts

Red Flag Toppings

- extra cheese
- pepperoni
- sausage
- anchovies
- bacon
- meatballs
- prosciutto
- mozzarella cheese

May I Take Your Order

Low-Calorie Sample Pizza Meal	**Greek salad** (green leaf lettuce with green pepper, tomato, and bits of feta cheese) *Quantity:* 2 cups *Exchanges:* 2 vegetable **Dressing:** 1 tablespoon Greek dressing (request lemon slices) *Exchanges:* 1 fat **Pizza** topped with green peppers, broccoli, and onions *Quantity:* 1 slice from large pizza *Exchanges:* 1 meat; 1 fat; 1 vegetable; 2 starch
Nutrition Summary	390 calories 35% calories as fat 19% calories as protein 46% calories as carbohydrate 50 mg cholesterol 720 mg sodium
Moderate-Calorie Sample Pizza Meal	**Special-request salad** (red leaf lettuce, green peppers, mushrooms, tomatoes, black olives, onion, sprinkle of mozzarella) *Quantity:* 2 cups *Exchanges:* 2 vegetable **Olive oil and vinegar dressing** (on the side) *Quantity:* 1 teaspoon oil; 2 tablespoons vinegar *Exchanges:* 1 fat (from the oil) **Pizza** topped with sauteed chicken strips, roasted peppers,

onions, white wine, oregano, feta
cheese
Quantity: 2 slices from large pizza
Exchanges: 3 meat; 2 fat; 2
vegetable; 4 starch

Nutrition
Summary

780	calories
36%	calories as fat
22%	calories as protein
42%	calories as carbohydrate
95	mg cholesterol
1170	mg sodium

Healthier eating out
Chinese Style

Chinese food is one of the most popular ethnic cuisines in America. Chinese foods, markets, and cookery were virtually unknown in America prior to the mid-1800s.

Initially, when people from China came to the United States, it was common for them to settle in enclaves that became known as "Chinatown." Chinatowns developed in several large coastal cities—Boston, New York, San Francisco. Today it is commonplace to find at least several Chinese restaurants in most American cities.

Americans are most accustomed to eating foods prepared in the Cantonese style. Now, beyond only Cantonese cuisine, there are restaurants that specialize in cuisine of various regions of China such as Szechuan, Hunan, and Peking (Beijing). There is varying opinion from different experts as to whether there are three, four, or five regional cuisines of China. In reality, there are many more if you discuss the many subtle regional differences. Many times, dishes on a Chinese menu will be named for that particular region: Peking duck, Szechuan spicy chicken, and Hunan crispy beef.

THE MENU PROFILE

No doubt Chinese food as it is eaten in China is healthier than in America. That is simply because the main focus for Americans is on protein; whereas, in China the main focus is on carbohydrates—white rice or noodles. Keep this in mind when you are ordering. Keep your focus on the carbos—the starches and vegetables.

A Chinese meal can easily match the nutrition goals recommended for everyone's improved health, that is, higher carbohydrates and less protein, fat, and sodium. In addition, Chinese food has the potential to be low in saturated fat and cholesterol. Rice and noodles are great carbohydrate sources. Vegetables, also primarily carbohydrate, are abundant in Chinese cooking. You are familiar with many of the vegetables used: broccoli, celery, carrots, and cabbage. Others are less familiar, such as bok choy, napa, wood ears, and lily buds (see Chinese Menu Lingo at the end of the chapter).

Fat is again one of the villains of Chinese cookery, but it is easy enough to pick and choose. Special requests are easily made to limit the fatty foods, added oils, and high-sodium sauces. Remember, to your advantage, most dishes are prepared to order.

Several foods higher in fat, such as duck, beef, and pork, can be limited. Many high-fat cuts of pork are used in Chinese cooking: spare ribs, for example. However, think of the roast pork strips appetizer that is quite lean. The biggest problem is the added fat used in cooking. There are many menu items, such as sweet-and-sour dishes, that are breaded and deep-fried and should be avoided. There are also several

Chinese appetizers to steer clear of—egg rolls, fried shrimp, and fried won tons.

The most common cooking method is stir-frying in a wok. In fact, it used to be rare to find an oven in China. A wok can also be used for other cooking methods such as braising and steaming. Wok cooking can be quite healthy. A minimal amount of oil can be used, and foods are cooked briefly so they retain vitamin and mineral content.

Traditionally, much lard (pork fat) was used in Chinese cooking, but according to some, more liquid oil is used today. Peanut oil is commonly used due to its high smoking point. Peanut oil also gives a slightly nutty flavor to dishes. It is mainly a monounsaturated fat, now thought to help lower blood cholesterol. Sesame seed oil is also used, but in smaller quantities. Sesame seed oil is a polyunsaturated fat, which also assists in lowering blood cholesterol. So, although oil used in Chinese cooking can be plentiful, the oils are healthy ones.

One other villain is the high sodium content of Chinese food. Many dishes contain high-sodium soy sauces, light and dark, and MSG (monosodium glutamate). Other sauces such as oyster, black bean, and hoisin also contain large amounts of sodium. For frame of reference, a tablespoon of soy sauce has about 1,000 milligrams of sodium, and the recommended daily intake is 3,000!

A few special requests can quickly decrease the sodium. You can request that less soy and no MSG be used. Many more Chinese restaurants today note on their menu that no MSG is used. Don't forget, all Chinese entrees are prepared to order, so special requests should be easy. I would not recommend eliminating soy altogether because the end product simply will be untasty. Think about using the sweet sauce, "duck" sauce, and hot mustard as low-sodium flavorings. However, Chinese food might not be the optimal choice, at least on a frequent basis, for individuals on a severely low-sodium diet.

You might wish to request that sugar be left out of your dishes if your blood sugar rises when you consume Chinese food. However, you might be told that it is already premixed into marinades or sauces. It is best to avoid sweet-and-sour dishes, the sweet sauces, hoisin and plum, and the sweet sauce on the table.

Green Flag Words

- lobster sauce
- cooked in light wine sauce
- simmered, steamed, roasted
- bean curd (tofu)
- with assorted vegetables: broccoli, mushrooms, onion, cabbage
- stir-fried in mild sauce
- hot and spicy tomato sauce
- served on a sizzling platter
- in slippery light sauce or velvet sauce
- garnished with spinach or broccoli
- fresh fish fillets

Red Flag Words

- fried, deep fried
- breaded and fried
- duck
- with cashews or peanuts
- pieces of egg
- egg foo young
- coated with water chestnut flour and fried
- crispy (usually means breaded and fried)
- dipped in batter and browned in oil
- served with a rich sweet sauce
- sweet-and-sour sauce
- served in bird's nest
- plum sauce
- soy sauce
- hoisin sauce

**Special Requests
Chinese Style**

- Please don't use MSG.
- What type of oil is used for stir-frying? (If lard or other saturated fat, request that peanut or other non-animal fat be used.)
- Would it be possible to use less oil in the preparation?
- Would it be possible to use less salt and soy sauce?
- Can you substitute chicken in this dish for duck?
- Could you substitute (or add in more) broccoli and leave out the spinach?
- Please don't garnish with peanuts or cashews.
- Can you leave off the crispy fried won ton?
- Please remove the crispy fried noodles from the table.

Typical Menu: Chinese Style

Appetizers

egg rolls
Spring rolls
✓ **Steamed Peking raviolis**
Peking raviolis
✓ **Roast pork strips**
Barbecued spare ribs
✓ **Teriyaki,** beef or chicken on skewers
Jumbo shrimp, fried
Won tons, fried

✓ indicates
preferred choices

Soups	✓ **Hot-and-sour**
	✓ **Won ton**
	✓ **Sizzling rice** and chicken or shrimp
	✓ **Delights of three** (assorted Chinese vegetables and chicken, pork, and beef strips)
	Egg drop
Poultry	✓ **Velvet chicken** (breast of chicken, snow peas, water chestnuts, bamboo shoots, and garnish of egg white)
	***General Gau's chicken** (cubes of chicken coated with water chestnut flour and eggs, deep fried until crispy, and coated with hot ginger sauce)
	Sweet-and-sour chicken (battered and fried, topped with a thick sweet-and-pungent sauce and pineapple)
	✓ **Chicken chop suey** (breast of chicken stir-fried with celery, Chinese cabbage, and assorted vegetables)
	✓ **Sizzling sliced chicken** with vegetables (sliced breast of chicken with assorted Chinese vegetables)
	✓ ***Yu Hsiang chicken** (strips of chicken stir-fried with bamboo shoots, water chestnuts, wood ears, lily buds, and Chinese cabbage)
	Sweet-and-pungent duck (cubes of duck, dipped in batter, deep

fried, and served with water chestnuts, cherries, and peas)

Seafood

✓ **Shrimp with broccoli** and mushrooms (stir-fried shrimp with broccoli and Chinese mushrooms in light egg white sauce)

*Spicy crispy whole fish** (a whole fish deep fried and coated with a hot, spicy sauce)

Shrimp and cashews (whole shrimp stir-fried with cashew nuts and water chestnuts)

✓ *Szechuan** style fresh fish fillets (fish fillets sauteed with bamboo shoots and scallions, served with a hot and spicy sauce)

✓ **Moo shi shrimp** (stir-fried shrimp with Chinese vegetables, served with Chinese pancakes and hoisin sauce)

Meats

✓ **Beef and broccoli** with black mushrooms (strips of beef sauteed with broccoli and black mushrooms in oyster sauce)

✓ *Twice cooked pork** (pork with cabbage, green peppers, and bamboo shoots in hot bean sauce)

*Hunan crispy beef** (beef deep fried and coated with a hot Hunan sauce, served with broccoli)

✓ **Roast pork** with vegetables (slices of pork stir-fried with assorted Chinese vegetables)

✔ **Beef chow mein** (sliced beef
stir-fried with diced cabbage,
onions, sliced mushrooms, and
other Chinese vegetables)

Vegetables

✔ **Vegetarian delight** (ten kinds of
crunchy vegetables stir-fried in a
light sauce)
***Yu Hsiang eggplant** (eggplant
stir-fried with other Chinese
vegetables)
✔ ***Spicy green beans** (green beans
sauteed in hot and spicy Hunan
sauce)
✔ **Broccoli** and black mushrooms in
oyster sauce

*Indicates a hot and spicy dish.

Rice

✔ **Steamed white rice**
Pork- or beef-fried rice
✔ **Vegetable-fried rice**

Noodles

Roast pork lo mein
✔ **Chicken lo mein**
✔ **Vegetable lo mein**
Pan-fried noodles with shrimp,
pork, and chicken
Pan-fried noodles with assorted
Chinese vegetables

Desserts

✔ **Pineapple chunks**
✔ **Lychee nuts**
Vanilla ice cream
Fried bananas served with sweet
syrup sauce
Fortune cookies

MAY I TAKE YOUR ORDER

Low-Calorie Sample Meal	**Hot-and-sour soup** *Quantity:* 1 cup *Exchanges:* 1 vegetable **Yu Hsiang chicken** *Quantity:* 1½ cups (split order) *Exchanges:* 2 meat; 1 fat; 1 vegetable **Shrimp with broccoli** and mushrooms (split order) *Quantity:* 1 cup *Exchanges:* 2 meat; 1 fat; 1 vegetable **Steamed white rice** *Quantity:* ⅔ cup *Exchanges:* 2 starch **Fortune cookie** (Read fortune; skip cookie)
Nutrition Summary	570 calories 35% calories as fat 29% calories as protein 36% calories as carbohydrate 150 mg cholesterol 1300 mg sodium +
Moderate-Calorie Sample Meal	**Peking raviolis,** steamed *Quantity:* 2 *Exchanges:* 1 starch; 1 meat; 1 fat; ½ vegetable **Moo shi shrimp** *Quantity:* 2 pancakes; 1½ cups filling (split order) *Exchanges:* 1 starch; 2 meat; 1 fat; 2 vegetable

Vegetable lo mein noodles
Quantity: 1½ cups (split order)
Exchanges: 3 starch; 1 fat; 1
vegetable
Tsing Tsao beer
Quantity: 12 oz.
Exchanges: 1 starch; 1 fat

Nutrition Summary	
911	calories
24%	calories as fat
19%	calories as protein
49%	calories as carbohydrate
8%	calories as alcohol
134	mg cholesterol
1300	mg sodium +

Chinese Menu Lingo

Bean curd—known as "tofu" to Americans; made from soy beans and formed into blocks; used sliced or cubed in soups or dishes. Be careful: it is often fried.

Black bean sauce—a thick, brown sauce made of fermented soy beans, salt, and wheat flour; frequently used in Cantonese cooking.

Bok choy—looks like a cross between celery and cabbage; also known as Chinese chard.

Five-spice powder—a reddish-brown powder, combining star anise, fennel, cinnamon, cloves, and Szechuan pepper; used in Szechuan dishes.

Hoisin sauce—a sweet and spicy thick sauce made from soy beans, sugar, garlic, chili, and vinegar. Served with moo shi dishes.

Lily buds—dried, golden-colored buds with a light, flowery flavor; also called lotus buds and tiger lily buds; used in entrees and soups.

Lychees—crimson-colored fruit with translucent flesh around a brown seed, closely resembling a white grape.

Monosodium glutamate (MSG)—a white powder used in small amounts to bring out and enhance the flavors of ingredients.

Napa—also referred to as Chinese cabbage, it has thick-ribbed stalks and crinkled leaves.

Oyster sauce—a rich, thick sauce made of oysters, their cooking liquid, and soy sauce; frequently used in Cantonese dishes.

Plum sauce—an amber-colored, thick sauce made from plums, apricots, hot peppers, vinegar, and sugar; it has a spicy sweet-and-sour flavor.

Sesame seed oil—oil extracted from sesame seeds; it has a strong sesame flavor and is used as seasoning for soups, seafood, and other dishes.

Soy sauce—either light or dark, used in virtually all Chinese dishes.

Sweet-and-sour sauce—thick sauce made from sugar, vinegar, and soy sauce. Meat, chicken, or shrimp served in this sauce usually has been dipped in batter and fried.

Wood ear—a variety of tree lichen, which is brown and resembles a wrinkled ear; it is soaked before use. Found in soups and some vegetable dishes.

6.

Healthier eating out
Thai Style

Americans are familiar with Chinese egg roll, chow mein, and moo shi but are comparative strangers to tod mun, shrimp choo chee, and pad Thai. These are frequent listings on ever-popular Thai menus.

Beyond simply our yen for great hot and spicy foods is an increasing knowledge that our eating habits are reflected in our health status. Thai food, generally speaking, fits into the healthy goals for eating—light on fats, meats, and sauces and heavy on carbos such as vegetables, noodles, and rice.

Thai cuisine is often compared with Chinese though the similarities do not go much beyond the stir-frying, the role of rice, and some similar ingredients. As for end results, Thai food differs substantially due to many different spices. In fact, taste-wise, Thai food more closely resembles Indian fare, with its use of aromatic flavors and spices—coriander, cumin, cardamom, cinnamon, to name a few. India and China are both Thailand's neighbors, so it is easy to see why both countries, as well as other Southeast Asian lands, have influenced Thai cooking. The food's appearance is as important as how it tastes.

THE MENU PROFILE

When looking over the menu to make selections, keep close tabs on the number of chili symbols or other notations alongside particular dishes. These indicate hot and spicy. Three notations means you had better have a glass of water within reach. The punch is contributed by spices and flavorings that have no calories or fat—so go ahead and be daring!

Due to the predominant role of rice, it is easy to keep the carbohydrates up. Another help in boosting carbos is that it is easy to find dishes with lots of veggies. There are always a few vegetarian offerings. Thus, it is easy to keep meat, poultry, or seafood portions down. It is not uncommon to see several seafood combination dishes. You will also see plenty of chicken and duck entrees. Duck is best to avoid due to its high fat content. If it is sliced duck with no skin, that is fine on occasion. In addition, beef and pork are the focus of many dishes. Both are fine choices as long as they are mixed with vegetables and balanced with seafood or vegetable dishes as the second or third entree ordered for sharing.

Though Thai cooking is generally light and healthy, some fat creeps in. It is easier to skirt the fried entrees than the appetizers, most of which are fried. Most often, entrees are stir-fried, steamed, boiled, or barbecued. Fat, as usual, is used in the wok. Hopefully, more often than not it is vegetable oil and not lard. You might want to ask and request the former.

Coconut milk is used quite a bit in Thai cuisine, and, unfortunately, similar to coconut oil, the milk is loaded with calories and saturated fat. A cup of canned coconut milk contains 445 calories, about 97% of which is fat. Certain dishes should be navigated around, such as the coconut-milk-laden curry entrees. If you eat a small quantity and do not eat Thai food all that often, a bit of coconut milk once in a while is not a problem.

The sodium content of Thai food can run high. The spicing and flavoring is not as dependent on soy sauces as in other Oriental cuisines. However, it is not uncommon to see soy sauce and/or salt added to main dishes, soups, rice (other than steamed), and noodle dishes. Some of the sauces, such as yellow bean paste, shrimp paste, and fish sauce, add some sodium.

It is best, as usual, to avoid the soups if you have been encouraged to keep sodium on the low side. Try requesting that less salt and/or soy be used in preparing your dishes. Also, to minimize sodium a bit more, request that no MSG be used.

People with diabetes should be advised that, in similar fashion to many Southeast Asian cuisines, a small amount of sugar is used in many dishes. Sometimes, Thais use palm sugar. If you feel that even a small amount of sugar makes your blood sugar rise, ask that the sugar be left out when the dish is prepared. On average, one teaspoon to two tablespoons of sugar might be added to a whole dish.

Green Flag Words
- stir-fried, sauteed, sizzling
- broiled, boiled, steamed
- braised, barbecued, charbroiled
- marinated
- basil sauce, basil, or sweet basil leaves
- lime sauce or lime juice
- chili sauce or crushed dried chili
- Thai spices
- served in a hollowed-out pineapple
- fish sauce
- hot sauce

- napa, bamboo shoots, black mushrooms, ginger, garlic
- bed of mixed vegetables
- scallions, onions

Red Flag Words

- sizzling deep-fried
- fried, deep-fried, crispy
- golden brown
- peanuts, cashews, peanut sauce
- curry sauce (often made with lots of coconut milk)
- made with coconut milk
- eggplant (most often fried)

Special Requests Thai Style

- Please hold the peanuts (or cashews) from this dish.
- Can you prepare these dishes with no MSG?
- What oil is used to prepare your foods? (If it's coconut oil or lard, ask that vegetable oil be used instead.)
- Please minimize the salt and soy sauce; I'm carefully watching my sodium consumption.
- Can I substitute scallops for shrimp or beef in this dish?
- Could I have a bit more broccoli and less beef in this dish?
- Could I get the rest of this wrapped up to take home; I'd like to enjoy it for dinner tomorrow night?
- Please put the dressing on the side of the salad.
- Please make this dish equivalent to three-chili hotness; I like lots of flavor.

Typical Menu: Thai Style

Appetizers

Thai spring rolls
(vegetable-filled; served with
sweet-and-sour sauce)

✓ **Satay** (beef or chicken marinated
in coconut milk and curry,
barbecued on skewers, and served
with peanut sauce and cucumber
salad)

Tod mun (minced shrimp and
codfish, mixed with Thai curry,
and fried until golden brown;
served with cucumber sauce)

✓ **Steamed mussels** (steamed with
lemon grass, sweet basil leaves,
chili, and Thai spices; served
with chili sauce)

✓ **Seafood kebab** (shrimp, scallops,
and vegetables on skewers, served
with hot sauce)

Soups

✓ **Tom yum koong** (Thai shrimp
soup with lemon grass, chili
paste, lime juice, and straw
mushrooms)

Tom ka gai (chicken in coconut
milk soup with mushrooms and
lime juice)

✓ **Crystal noodle** (clear soup with
chicken, bean-thread noodles,
and vegetables)

✓ indicates
preferred choices

Salads	✓ **Thai salad** (green mixed garden salad with tofu and egg wedges, dressed with spiced peanut sauce)
	✓ **Pla koong** (spicy shrimp salad with onion, scallions, tomatoes, mushrooms, lemon grass, all tossed with chili and lime juice)
	✓ **Yam yai** (spicy combination salad of shrimp, pork, and chicken with lettuce, cucumber, onion, and tomato in light spicy dressing)
Curry	The following curry dishes can be made with either chicken, beef, shrimp, scallops, tofu, or vegetables.
	✓ ***Green curry** (in coconut milk, with bamboo shoots, green peppers, string beans, green peas, and zucchini)
	✓ ***Red curry** (in coconut milk, with bamboo shoots, red and green peppers)
	*Note comments in text about coconut milk.
Poultry	**Crispy duck** (fried duck, steamed with soy sauce, topped with fried spinach, and served with plum sauce)
	✓ **Chili duck** (sauteed roast duck with onion, hot pepper, mushrooms, scallions, and fresh sweet basil leaves with spiced tomato sauce)
	✓ **Thai chicken** (chicken sauteed with cashews, onions,

mushrooms, pineapple, scallions, and chili; served in a whole pineapple)
Chicken in the garden (boiled, sliced chicken on a bed of broccoli, carrots, cauliflower, green beans, and asparagus; topped with peanut sauce)

Beef/Pork

*Spareribs curry (red curry in coconut milk, with boneless spareribs, peas, string beans, snowpeas, hot pepper, tomato, and sweet basil leaves)
✓ **Beef basil** (sauteed beef flavored with hot basil leaves, fresh hot pepper, mushrooms, and red pepper)
Praram long song (fried beef with special curry sauce and peanuts over a bed of spinach)
✓ **Ginger pork** (sauteed pork in ginger with green pepper, onion, scallions, mushrooms, and chili paste)

Seafood

Hot Thai catfish (deep-fried catfish fillet topped with bamboo shoots, baby corn, mushrooms, eggplant, hot chili, and basil leaves with Thai spices)
✓ **Garlic shrimp** (sauteed shrimp with fresh garlic, peppercorns, snowpeas, and napa; served on a bed of sliced cucumbers)
✓ **Poy sian** (combination of seafood sauteed with straw mushrooms,

napa, bamboo shoots, onions, and
string beans)

✓ **Scallops bamboo** (sauteed sea
scallops with bamboo shoots,
snowpeas, baby corn, mushrooms,
and scallions all mixed with Thai
spices)

Vegetables　　**Royal tofu** (deep-fried pieces of
tofu with snowpeas, onions,
scallions, and broccoli seasoned
with a spicy chili sauce)

✓ **Pad jay** (combination of napa,
celery, onions, carrots,
mushrooms, and bean sprouts
topped with a sauce of Thai
spices)

Rice and Noodles　　**Fried rice** (rice fried with
chicken, scallions, green peas,
onion, and egg)

Vegetable fried rice (rice fried
with assorted stir-fry vegetables)

✓ **Steamed rice**

✓ **Pad Thai** (noodles stir-fried with
ground peanuts, bean sprouts,
egg, tofu, and scallions, topped
with shrimp)

Desserts　　✓ **Lychee nuts**

Fried banana (deep-fried banana
served with a sweet syrup sauce)

Thai custard

May I Take Your Order

Low-Calorie Sample Meal	**Tom yum koong** *Quantity:* 1 cup *Exchanges:* ½ meat; ½ vegetable **Thai chicken** (hold cashews) *Quantity:* 1 cup *Exchanges:* 2 meat (lean); 1 fat; 1 vegetable **Poy Sian** *Quantity:* 1 cup *Exchanges:* 2 meat (lean); 1 fat; 1 vegetable **Steamed rice** *Quantity:* 1 cup *Exchanges:* 3 starch **Mineral water** *Quantity:* 12 oz. *Exchanges:* free
Nutrition Summary	528 calories 29% calories as fat 22% calories as protein 49% calories as carbohydrate 153 mg cholesterol 1210 mg sodium
Moderate-Calorie Sample Meal	**Green curry with tofu** *Quantity:* 1½ cups *Exchanges:* 2 fat; 3 vegetable **Scallops bamboo** *Quantity:* 1½ cups *Exchanges:* 3 meat (lean); 1 fat; 2 vegetable **Pad Thai** *Quantity:* 1 cup

Exchanges: ½ meat (lean); 2 fat; 2 starch
Steamed rice
Quantity: ⅔ cup
Exchanges: 2 starch
Coffee
Quantity: 2 cups
Exchanges: free

Nutrition Summary	818 calories
	35% calories as fat
	23% calories as protein
	42% calories as carbohydrate
	64 mg cholesterol
	1260 mg sodium

Thai Menu Lingo

Bamboo shoots—an oriental vegetable commonly found in Thai entrees; light in color, crunchy, and stringy in texture and very low in calories.

Basil—*horapa*, as it's known in Thailand, basil is used mainly in leaf form; there are several types of basil used in Thai cooking.

Cardamom—a member of the ginger family, the seeds are often used in curry mixtures and other dishes, as seeds or ground.

Chilies—various types used, depending on hotness of dish; red and green are common, used whole, chopped, or ground into paste for sauces.

Coconut milk—liquid extracted from grating fresh coconut, not the liquid from inside the coconut; used in marinating and in gravies for various dishes, especially curry sauces.

Coriander—dried coriander seed is the main ingredient in curry mixtures; the seeds or leaves are used; an essential spice in Thai cooking.

Cumin—another fragrant spice important to curry mixtures, used either as seeds or ground.

Curry—really a combination of spices, not a single spice as known in the U.S.; different spice and food combinations create the green, red, and mussaman curry mixtures.

Kapi—dried shrimp paste made from prawns or shrimp, commonly used to flavor many Thai dishes.

Lemon grass—*takrai*, as it's known in Thailand, is an Asian plant whose bulbous base is used to add a lemony flavor to many soups and main entrees.

Lime—*makrut*, in Thai, lime leaves or the juice of kaffir lime is commonly used in soups, salads, and entrees.

Nam pla—a fish sauce used like soy sauce in Thai cooking; this thin, salty brown sauce brings out the flavor of other foods.

Nam prik—called Thai shrimp sauce, it is used to flavor many Thai foods; made from shrimp paste, chilies, lime juice, soy sauce, and sugar.

Napa—also referred to as Chinese cabbage, it has thick-ribbed stalks and crinkled leaves.

Palm sugar—a strong-flavored, dark sugar obtained from the sap of coconut palms; it is boiled down until it crystallizes.

Scallions—also called spring onions, they are white, slender, and have long green stems; usually they are chopped into small pieces.

Soy sauce—used in many Thai dishes to cast a salty flavor; made from soy beans.

Tamarind—an acidy-tasting fruit from a large tropical tree; used for its acid flavor.

Turmeric—the spice that lends the yellow-orange color to commercial curry; part of the ginger family.

Healthier eating out
Japanese Style

When Japanese restaurants are mentioned, many people form images of Japanese steak houses. These so-called Japanese, but relatively Americanized, restaurants serve the familiar tempura, sukiyaki, and teriyaki. There is usually a talented Japanese chef cooking or, more correctly, performing in front of you.

These restaurants still abound. There are, however, many smaller, more authentic Japanese restaurants serving such foreign-sounding but familiar Japanese items as agemono, yosenabe, and donburi.

THE MENU PROFILE

Japanese cuisine accents carbohydrates in rice and vegetables and minimizes fats by using food preparation methods that require little or no oil or fat. In addition, small portions are the standard in Japanese fare.

The higher than desirable sodium level of Japanese food is mainly contributed by the soy-based items. Marinades and sauces, whether for teriyaki, sukiyaki, or shabu-shabu, are a combination of some or all of the following: shoyu, dashi, mirin, sugar, sake, and a bit of kombu.

Unfortunately, if you order a dish such as teriyaki, you can be assured that the protein, whether it is meat or fish, has been prepared in the high-sodium sauce. However, if you order a dish such as shabu-shabu, you can closely control the amount of sauce used because this dish is cooked at the table and you do the dipping.

Basically, in a Japanese restaurant the only fat you end up with on your plate is from the foods you have chosen. Therefore, ordering fish, shellfish, or poultry rather than selecting beef or pork helps keep the fat count down. The size of the portions, whether it is fish or beef, seems to be more in line with healthy guidelines, too, than a typical American meal.

If fats are used in Japanese cookery, they are mainly the no-cholesterol varieties such as cottonseed, olive, peanut, or sesame seed oil. Sesame seed oil is used in minimal quantity for its wonderful nutty flavor.

It is typical to see sugar incorporated into Japanese food preparation on a regular basis, as is true in most Southeast Asian cuisines. Sugar is used in almost all the sauces and marinades. Sugar is found in su, or "vinegared" rice, used in sushi. Su rice is flavored with vinegar, salt, and sugar although it is just referred to as vinegared rice.

In the end, most sauces and dishes will not provide you with more than several teaspoons to a tablespoon of sugar. However, it is important that you recognize that sugar is used if that is a concern.

The regularly served raw seafood dishes, sushi and sashimi, have gained popularity in the United States. They have become "in foods." Certainly, sushi and sashimi have a long heritage in Japanese dining.

A few words to the wise about the safety of eating raw seafood are included in the seafood chapter.

There are various types of sushi, and many different fish, shellfish, and vegetables are used in its creation. Great importance is placed on the freshness of the fish and the creativity with which these foods are served. Sushi, which is just a general term for a combination of raw seafood and vinegared rice (su), is served in a variety of ways. Either in, around, or under the fish you will find vinegared rice. Served with sushi are wasabi, a strong, green-color horseradish paste, and a soy-based sauce for dipping.

Sashimi is more simply served but with no less attention to freshness and beauty. Sashimi is raw, sliced fish served on small shallow dishes. It is served with a cone of wasabi, grated ginger root, and soy-based dipping sauce. Tuna, salmon, lobster, clams, and bream are commonly used for sashimi.

Calorically speaking, both sushi and sashimi are smart choices if you enjoy raw fish. They can be ordered as an appetizer or used as a main course. If desired, sashimi can be complemented with a bowl of steamed rice and tossed salad with miso dressing; the result is a low-fat and relatively low-sodium meal.

Green Flag Words

- steamed (mushimono)
- sauteed, braised, simmered, boiled
- broiled (yaki), barbecued, grilled (yakimono)
- clear broth
- marinated
- vinegared (usually with vinegar, salt, and sugar)
- seasoned rice
- vinegar sauce*
- on skewers
- teriyaki sauce*, dipping sauce*
- miso*, miso dressing*

• served in broth*
*Usually high in sodium content;
carefully monitor quantity used.

Red Flag Words

• deep-fried, battered (or
breaded) and fried
• tempura
• agemono
• katsu
• fried bean curd
• pan-fried

**Special Requests
Japanese Style**

• Could you serve the salad with
the dressing on the side?
• I'm carefully watching my salt
intake; can you use less sauce in
preparing this dish?
• Could you substitute shrimp,
scallops, or chicken for the beef
in this dish?
• Could you leave the egg out of
the sukiyaki (or donburi)?
• I couldn't finish all this; may I
get it wrapped up to take home?

Typical Menu: Japanese Style

**Sashimi and
Sushi**

✓ **Sashimi, tuna** (fillet of fresh raw
tuna served with wasabi and
dipping sauce)

✓ **Sashimi, combination** (fillet of
fresh raw seafood, tuna, salmon,
and lobster, with wasabi and

✓ indicates
preferred choices   dipping sauce)

✔ **Chirashi sushi** (fresh raw seafood served on seasoned rice, with pickled vegetables and seaweed)

✔ **Maki sushi** (fresh raw tuna and vinegared rice rolled in seaweed)

Appetizers

✔ **Yutofu** (hot bean curd boiled with napa, served with special sauce)

✔ **Ebi-su** (shrimp in vinegar sauce)

✔ **Shumai** (steamed shrimp dumplings wrapped in thin noodle skin)

Tempura appetizer (shrimp and vegetables dipped in batter and lightly fried)

✔ **Yakitori** (two skewers of chicken broiled with teriyaki sauce)

Agedashi tofu (fried tofu in tempura sauce)

✔ **Ohitashi** (fresh spinach boiled and served with soy sauce)

Soups

✔ **Suimono** (clear broth soup)

✔ **Miso** (soy bean paste soup with tofu and scallions)

✔ **Su-udon** (plain Japanese noodle soup)

Tempura-udon (Japanese noodle soup with tempura)

✔ **Yaki-udon** (Japanese noodle soup with stir-fried vegetables)

Salads

✔ **Tossed salad** served with miso dressing

✔ **Tofu salad** served with miso dressing

✓ **Seafood sunomono** (seafood with cucumber, seaweed, and shredded garnish with vinegar sauce)

Entrees

Entrees served à la carte with steamed white rice or soba noodles

Tempura (lightly battered and fried; served with tempura sauce). Choice of: Shrimp; Vegetable; Combination shrimp and vegetable

Teriyaki (broiled and served with teriyaki sauce). Choice of: ✓ chicken; ✓ beef; ✓ salmon

Agemono (battered in breadcrumbs and deep-fried). Choice of: Tonkatsu (pork cutlet); Chicken katsu; Shrimp

✓ **Sukiyaki,** Chicken or Beef (with tofu, bamboo shoots, and vegetables simmered in sukiyaki sauce)

✓ **Yosenabe** (noodles, seafood, and vegetables simmered in a special broth)

✓ **Shabu-shabu** (sliced beef and vegetables with noodles cooked and served at the table, with dipping sauces)

Donburi (served on a bed of rice with special sauce). Choice of: ✓ Oyako (sauteed chicken, egg, and onion); Katsu (deep-fried breaded pork, egg, onion); Unagi (broiled eel)

Desserts   ✓ **Fresh fruit**
                    Ice cream, ginger or vanilla
                    Yo kan (sweet bean cake)

May I Take Your Order

Low-Calorie   **Sashimi, tuna**
Sample Meal   *Quantity:* 1 serving
                    Exchanges: 3 meat (lean)
                    Dipping sauce for above
                    Quantity: 2 tablespoons
                    Exchanges: free
                    Yaki-udon soup
                    Quantity: 1 cup
                    Exchanges: 1 fat; 1 vegetable; 1
                    starch
                    Steamed rice
                    Quantity: 1 cup
                    Exchanges: 3 starch
                    Tofu salad (dressing on the side)
                    Quantity: 1–2 cups
                    Exchanges: ½ meat (lean); 1–2
                    vegetables
                    Miso dressing for above (on the
                    side)
                    Quantity: 2 tablespoons
                    Exchanges: free

Nutrition   528 calories
Summary   16% calories as fat
                     30% calories as protein
                     54% calories as carbohydrate
                      76 mg cholesterol
                    1490 mg sodium

Moderate-Calorie Sample Meal	**Ohitashi**
	Quantity: 1 order
	Exchanges: 1 vegetable
	Suimono soup
	Quantity: 1 cup
	Exchanges: 1 vegetable
	Teriyaki, salmon (split order)
	Quantity: 4 oz.
	Exchanges: 4 meat (lean)
	Donburi, oyako (split order)
	Quantity: 1½ cups
	Exchanges: 1 meat (medium); 3 starch
	Steamed rice
	Quantity: ⅔ cup
	Exchanges: 2 starch
	Fresh fruit
	Quantity: 1 small piece
	Exchanges: 1 fruit

Nutrition Summary	
719	calories
23%	calories as fat
30%	calories as protein
47%	calories as carbohydrate
251	mg cholesterol (mainly from egg in Donburi)
1700	mg sodium

Japanese Menu Lingo

Bonito—a fish important in Japanese cuisine; a member of the mackerel family; bonito flakes are an important ingredient in the basic stock called dashi.

Daikon—giant white radish; grated daikon is mixed into tempura sauces.

Dashi—an important element in Japanese cooking, dashi is the basic stock made with water, kombu (seaweed), and bonito flakes.

Gyuniku—beef.

Kombu—a Japanese seaweed central to the basic stock, dashi; also used in sauces and as a wrapper for certain dishes.

Mirin—Japanese rice wine, which is used more in sauces than consumed as a beverage; a central ingredient to the sauces and flavors of Japanese cuisine.

Miso—a fermented soy bean paste that comes in various types, thicknesses, and degrees of saltiness; used in soups, sauces, and dressings—a basic ingredient in Japanese cooking.

Nori—a seaweed often toasted prior to using; has a strong flavor and is used to wrap maki sushi.

Sake—fermented rice wine, sake is the national alcoholic beverage of Japan, most often served warm; it is also used as an ingredient in sauces.

Shitake mushrooms—an abundant mushroom in Japanese cookery, it has a woody and fruity flavor; used fresh or dried.

Shoyu—Japanese soy sauce, with light or dark varieties; it is made from soy beans, wheat, and salt and is an essential ingredient in Japanese cooking.

Teriyaki sauce—sauce used to broil; made from shoyu and mirin. Teriyaki means "shining broil."

Tofu—soy bean curd, a major source of protein in the Japanese diet; used in soups, salads, and entrees.

Ton—pork.

Tori—chicken.

Vinegar—in Japan, made from rice and lighter and sweeter than the vinegar Americans are used to.

Wakame—a seaweed used for its flavor and texture; available dried.

Wasabi—grated horseradish that is fragrant and sharp in taste; one of the strongest spices used in Japanese cooking, it is commonly served with raw fish.

8.

Healthier eating out
Indian Style

Raita, or rayta, dahl, or dall, nan, and biryani. These
are just a sampling of commonly served foods in most
Asian Indian restaurants. They do not have the
familiar ring of a burger, fries, and Coke. One of the
first challenges of learning how to enjoy healthy dining in an Indian restaurant is to acquire the language
of Asian Indian cuisine. Take a glance through the
Indian Menu Lingo at chapter's end.

One simply has to look at India's location on a
map of the world for clues about the tastes you can
expect. Though Indian food has many unique qualities and cooking techniques, it more closely resembles the cuisine of neighboring Pakistan, Sri Lanka,
Thailand, and Burma. A bit more distant is China,
with which there are a few similarities. To Americans, Indian food most closely resembles Thai food,
both in similarity of spices and ingredients. Curries
are commonly served in both countries. They can be
quite hot and spicy. Rice is a predominant feature of
both cuisines. Basmati rice is the rice of choice in
India.

THE MENU PROFILE

As with most ethnic cuisines, there are pros and cons to Indian cookery. If you have some basic knowledge of the cuisine, are careful about reading the food descriptions, and ask questions, you will have no problem.

The pros of Indian foods include its accent on carbohydrates and deemphasis of protein. Basmati rice, the premier rice, is a main element of Indian cuisine. Breads are considered an important part of the meal, although one needs to watch out for the fried varieties. Legumes, including lentils and chick peas, are often found in dishes or accompaniments. These are good sources of soluble fiber and non-animal protein. Vegetables are incorporated into most meals. They might be in curry dishes, biryani, and pullao. Commonly served Indian vegetables are spinach, eggplant, cabbage, potatoes, and peas. Onions, green peppers, and tomatoes are often found in the stewed entrees. Yogurt is frequently used in gravies; it is the plain variety.

Another positive aspect that assists in keeping protein, calories, and cholesterol low is the wide availability of chicken and seafood. Beef and lamb are commonly found on the menu but can easily be avoided. Pork and pork products are rarely found on Indian menus. Small quantities of protein are used. This likely relates back to their minimal availability. If two people share a chicken or shrimp massala, one won't eat much more than two to three ounces of protein. Also, it is a great idea to order one chicken or seafood dish and one vegetable dish, maybe a biryani or aloo chole, to keep the calories and fat low.

A garam massala, or fragrant mix of ground spices, produces many of the wonderful tastes of Indian cuisine. Some spices frequently found in the garam massala are cardamom, coriander, cumin, cloves, and cinnamon. Several of these spices are referred to as "fragrant" spices. In the southern regions, you might find pepper and chilies added to raise the "heat." Mint, garlic, ginger, yogurt, and coconut milk are other common ingredients in Indian cooking. You will find more of these spices and ingredients defined in the Indian Menu Lingo section at the end of this chapter.

The negative aspects of Indian cuisine can be the high fat content. Fat finds its way into Indian foods by way of food preparation. Ghee, defined as clarified butter, is a common ingredient. Frying and sauteing are common preparation methods. For example, most appetizers, such as samosa and pakora, are fried. Many breads are fried, such as paratha and poori.

The oils most frequently used in Indian cooking are sesame and coconut oil. Sesame is mainly a polyunsaturated oil. However, coconut oil is about the most saturated oil one can use. You might want to ask about the oil in use, and if it is coconut oil, avoid the fried food to reduce calories as well as saturated fat.

There is a wide use of coconut milk in Indian cooking, and this, too, contributes calories, fat, and saturated fat. Look for the words coconut milk, coconut cream, or simply shredded coconut in the descriptions of menu items and try to avoid these.

The sodium content of an Indian meal can be kept within bounds by navigating around the menu carefully. It is best to avoid the soups, which tend to be high in sodium. Many dishes have small amounts of salt added, but if it is divided into a number of servings and you keep the portions small, you will consume a minimal quantity.

Green Flag Words

- tikka (pan roasted)
- cooked with or marinated in yogurt
- cooked with green vegetables
- cooked with onions, tomatoes, spinach, peppers, and/or mushrooms
- baked leavened bread

- masala
- tandoori
- paneer
- cooked with curry
- marinated or cooked in spices
- chick peas, potatoes, lentils
- basmati rice (pullao)
- matta (peas)
- kebab

Red Flag Words

- dipped in batter
- deep fried, fried, fritters
- korma
- stuffed and fried
- creamy curry sauce
- ghee
- garnished with nuts
- cooked in cream sauce
- molee (coconut)
- coconut milk or soup

Special Requests Indian Style

- Please bring the accompaniments raita, dahl, and onion chutney.
- If a special rice is ordered, request that the plain pullao not be brought.
- My order will be *à la carte*, not a complete dinner.
- Please don't garnish with nuts or dried fruits.
- Is it possible to prepare my dish without adding any salt?
- Please bring my salad (or soup) when the others have their appetizers.
- I'll have a cup of Darjeeling tea with my meal.

Typical Menu: Indian Style

Appetizers

Cheese pakoras (homemade cheese deep-fried in chick pea batter)

✔ **Samosa** (vegetable turnover, stuffed and fried)

Fried shrimp with poori (shrimp with onions and peppers, fried with spices)

✔ **Papadum,** or papad (crispy, thin lentil wafers)

Soups

✔ **Mulligatawny** (lentil, vegetables, and spices)

Coconut soup (coconut cream and pistachio nuts)

✔ **Dahl rasam** (pepper soup with lentils)

Breads (Roti)

Paratha (shallow-fried multi-layered bread made with butter)

Poori (light, puffed fried bread)

✔ **Chapati** (thin, dry whole-wheat bread)

✔ **Nan** (leavened baked bread topped with poppy seeds)

✔ indicates preferred choices

Chicken (Murgi)	✓ **Chicken tandoori** (marinated in spices and roasted in a tandoor, or clay oven)
	✓ **Chicken tikka** (roasted in charcoal oven with mild spices)
	✓ **Chicken vandaloo** (boneless chicken cooked with potatoes and hot spices)
	Chicken kandhari (chicken cooked with cream sauce and cashews)
	✓ **Chicken masala** (roasted chicken cooked in spices and thick curry sauce)
Shrimp/Fish	**Shrimp malai** (cooked with cream, mushrooms, and coconut)
	✓ **Shrimp bhuna** (cooked with green vegetables, onions, and tomatoes)
	✓ **Fish masala** (boneless fish marinated in a spicy yogurt sauce)
	Shrimp curry (cooked in a thick curry sauce)
Beef/Lamb	✓ **Lamb bhuna** (pan roasted with spices, onions, and tomatoes)
	✓ **Lamb saag** (cooked with spinach in a spicy curry sauce)
	✓ **Beef vandaloo** (beef curry cooked with potatoes and hot spices)
	Beef korma (beef curry cooked with cream)

Rice (Pullao)	✓ **Shrimp biryani** (shrimp cooked with basmati rice)
	✓ **Vegetable biryani** (basmati rice cooked with green vegetables)
	✓ **Plain pullao** (basmati rice cooked with saffron)
	✓ **Peas pullao** (basmati rice cooked with peas)
Vegetables	✓ **Vegetable curry** (green peas, tomatoes, and cauliflower)
	Vegetable korma (mixed vegetables cooked with cream, herbs, and cashews)
	✓ **Saag paneer** (spinach cooked with homemade cheese)
	✓ **Aloo chole** (chick peas cooked with tomatoes and potatoes)
Accompaniments	✓ **Raita** (yogurt with grated cucumbers, onions, and spices)
	✓ **Mango chutney**
	Mint chutney
	✓ **Onion chutney** (diced onions with hot spices)
	Dahl (bean-based sauce)
	✓ **Tamata salat** (diced tomatoes and onions with hot spices and lemon)
Desserts	**Koulfi** (rich ice cream with almonds and pistachios)
	Gulab jamun (fried milk balls soaked in sugar syrup, served warm)
	Ras malai (homemade cheese in sweetened milk)

May I Take Your Order

Low-Calorie Sample Meal

Nan
Quantity: ¼ loaf
Exchanges: 1 fat; 1 starch
Shrimp biryani
Quantity: 1½ cups
Exchanges: 2 meat; 1 fat; 1 vegetable; 2 starch
Raita
Quantity: 3 tablespoons
Exchanges: ½ vegetable
Onion chutney
Quantity: 2 tablespoons
Exchanges: ½ vegetable
Tamata salat
Quantity: ½ cup
Exchanges: 1 vegetable
Darjeeling tea
Quantity: 2 cups
Exchanges: free

Nutrition Summary

480 calories
25% calories as fat
24% calories as protein
50% calories as carbohydrate
128 mg cholesterol
950 mg sodium

Moderate-Calorie Sample Meal

Samosa
Quantity: 1 piece
Exchanges: 2 fat; 1 starch
Chicken tandoori
Quantity: 4 oz. (split order)
Exchanges: 4 meat (lean); 1 fat

Peas pullao
Quantity: 1½ cups
Exchanges: 3 starch
Saag paneer
Quantity: 1 cup
Exchanges: 1 fat; 2 vegetable; ½ milk
Mint chutney
Quantity: 2 tablespoons
Exchanges: free
Dahl
Quantity: 3 tablespoons
Exchanges: ½ starch

Nutrition Summary	
852	calories
38%	calories as fat
23%	calories as protein
39%	calories as carbohydrate
93	mg cholesterol
1700	mg sodium

Indian Menu Lingo

Bombay duck—this term does not describe a bird but rather fish served either sauteed, fried, or dried, along with curries and rice; not often seen on U.S. Indian menus.

Cardamom—expensive spice native to India, in the ginger family. Either the whole cardamom pod or only seeds are used; one of the most common spices found in garam masalas (curry mixtures).

Cinnamon—delicate spice commonly found in spice combinations used in curries and rarely as the ground spice typically used in the U.S.; stick cinnamon with more intense flavor is used in India.

Clove—another commonly used spice in curries, it is the dried flower bud of an evergreen tropical tree found in Southeast Asia.

Coconut milk—not the liquid found inside the coconut, it is a creamy fluid extracted from the flesh of the coconut.

Coriander—fragrant spice often the main ingredient in curries; either ground coriander or the whole leaf is used. Also called cilantro or Chinese parsley.

Cumin—another fragrant spice important to curry dishes; used as either seeds or ground.

Curry—"curry" is not an individual spice in Indian cooking. The word means "sauce," and many spices, individually roasted, make up the curry mixture, known as garam masala.

Fennel—another spice used in curries; a member of the cumin family and on occasion referred to as sweet cumin.

Ghee—clarified butter; contains none of the milk solids.

Malai—a thick cream made by separating and collecting the top part of boiled milk; used in entrees for a thick, creamy sauce.

Mint—used to add flavor to curry dishes and also as a main ingredient in mint chutney and mint sambal; used in biryani and as a dipping sauce for appetizers.

Paneer—referred to as homemade cream or cottage cheese and made from milk curdled with lemon juice and strained through cheesecloth. Paneer is used in vegetable and rice dishes. For vegetarians, it is a complete protein source.

Poppy seeds—ground to a powder and used in curry dishes to thicken the gravies.

Rose water—flavoring agent used in Indian desserts; extracted from rose petals by steaming and then diluting the essence.

Saffron—known as the most expensive spice in the world, small quantities are used commonly in Indian cooking. Obtained by drying the stamens of saffron crocus, saffron strands are thread-like and deep orange in color.

Tamarind—used for its acidic quality, it is a fruit from a large tropical tree; a commonly used Indian spice or food.

Turmeric—spice which lends the yellow-orange color to commercial curry. Part of the ginger family and commonly used in Indian cooking.

Yogurt—a common ingredient in Indian cooking; always plain and unflavored.

9.

Healthier eating out
Middle Eastern Style

Pita bread, hummus, and baba ghanoush are becoming familiar foods in America. Middle Eastern restaurants are not as plentiful, especially in the heartland of America, as Italian or Chinese but the number is on the rise. Over the last century, more Middle Easterners have emigrated to the U. S., and, as usual, this pattern has resulted in an increase of restaurants.

Let's define what is meant by "Middle Eastern cuisine." There are strong similarities among the foods native to Greece, Syria, Lebanon, Iran, Iraq, Turkey, Armenia, and Israel. There are also commonalities to North Africa, the countries of Morocco, Egypt, Tunisia, Algeria, and Libya.

THE MENU PROFILE

As usual, the foods that play a predominant role in Middle Eastern cooking are those naturally plentiful in that region. Wheat, grains, legumes, olives, dates, figs, lamb, and eggplant are just a few of the ingredients central to Middle Eastern cooking.

Rice, combined with a variety of ingredients to make rice pilaf, is commonly served in Greece and the Middle East, whereas couscous, made with cracked wheat, is indigenous to North African countries. Tabooli, the cold cracked wheat or bulghur salad marinated with raw vegetables, is most familiar in Lebanon, though served throughout the Middle East.

Pita pockets, as they're called in America, are flat, round breads only slightly leavened. Due to the very hot oven in which they are cooked, steam is created, and the process results in a hollow center. This "pocket" is perfect for stuffing.

It is common to find stuffed dishes. Probably the best known are dolma, stuffed grape leaves. There are also stuffed cabbage and stuffed eggplant. They all can be stuffed with meat or vegetarian mixtures.

Chick peas, fava beans, and other legumes are indigenous to the Middle East. Chick peas and fava beans are pureed together to make falafel or ta'amia. Chick peas are mashed and mixed with tahini (sesame seed paste or puree) to make the familiar hummus.

Due to the plentifulness of olives, olive oil is frequently the product of choice. It is often used in cold dishes. Olives, both green and black, are frequently served. These very salty olives, which are soaked in brine, are called kalamata.

There is minimal seafood in Middle Eastern cookery. Other than legumes and grains, lamb is the most familiar meat. Beef is also used but to a lesser degree. Eggs are used quite a bit.

Milk is not frequently drunk in the Middle East due in part to the high incidence of lactose intolerance. Yogurt is frequently used, served plain as a side dish or mixed with garlic, mint, and salt. Yogurt might be found as a dressing for salads, in soups, or as a base in sauces such as tzateki. The purpose of yogurt, as in Indian cuisine, is to act as a palate refresher, or soother from the spiciness. Two cheeses, feta and kasseri, are commonly used in Middle Eastern cookery, served alone or incorporated into appetizers, salads, and entrees.

Phyllo (also filo or fila), which literally means leaf, is the paper-thin Middle Eastern dough. It is used to make sweet desserts, such as baklava, or dinner pies, such as spanikopita, the well-known spinach and feta cheese dish.

The geographic locale has an impact on ingredients, spices, and flavors of the foods served. Commonly used spices are parsley, mint, cilantro, and oregano. Others include spices that are also mainstays in Indian cooking—cumin, coriander, cinnamon, and ginger. Long ago, the Middle East was a major link on the spice route between the East and Europe.

Green Flag Words

- lemon dressing, lemon juice
- blended or seasoned with Middle Eastern spices
- herbs, herbs and spices
- mashed chick peas
- fava beans
- with tomatoes, onions, green peppers, and/or cucumbers
- spiced ground meat
- special garlic sauce
- basted with tomato sauce
- garlic
- chopped parsley and/or onion
- cracked wheat
- grape vines or leaves
- stuffed with ground lamb or meat
- stuffed with rice and imported spices
- grilled on a skewer

- marinated and barbecued
- baked, or charcoal broiled
- stewed or simmered

Red Flag Words

- caviar+
- tahini
- sesame paste or puree
- olive oil, pure olive oil
- eggs
- kalamata (olives)*
- feta cheese*
- kasseri cheese
- lokaniko*
- tarator sauce
- lemon and butter sauce
- cheese pie
- bechamel sauce
- in pastry crust
- phyllo dough
- pan fried, golden fried

  High in sodium in addition to fat
  + High in sodium and cholesterol

Special Requests Middle Eastern Style

- Please bring my salad dressing on the side.
- Please serve the tzateki (or other sauces) on the side.
- Please bring my salad (or soup) when you bring the appetizers for the others.
- I'll have the appetizer portion, but serve it when you bring the others their entrees.
- We're simply going to have salad and share a few appetizers.
- Can you leave the feta cheese and olives off the salad? I'm

watching my sodium consumption.
- Please bring an extra plate because we're going to do some sharing.
- Could I get a doggie bag when you bring the entrees? I'd like to put half away for tomorrow.

Typical Menu: Middle Eastern Style

Appetizers

✓ **Hummus bi tahini** with pita bread (mashed chick peas blended with tahini, lemon juice, and spices)

✓ **Baba ghanoush** with pita bread (smoked eggplant mashed and combined with tahini, lemon juice, garlic, and other spices)

Taramosalata with pita bread (caviar blended with lemon juice and olive oil)

Kasseri casserole (kasseri cheese fried with a lemon and butter sauce)

Spanikopita (spinach and feta cheese pie made with phyllo dough)

✓ **Dolma** (cold grape leaves stuffed with a spicy combination of rice, onions, and tomatoes)

Falafel (blend of chick peas and fava beans, fried and served with tarator or tahini)

✓ indicates preferred choices

Salads	✓ **Greek salad** (lettuce, tomato, cucumbers, onions, feta cheese, and olives, served with a light lemon and olive oil dressing)
	✓ **Tabooli** (cracked wheat combined with parsley, tomatoes, cucumbers, lemon, and a spicy dressing)
	✓ **Fattoush** (lettuce, peppers, scallions, onions, tomatoes, and pieces of toasted pita bread, tossed and served with a light garlic and lemon dressing)
Soups	**Avgolemono** (chicken-broth based soup with eggs and lemon)
	✓ **Lentil soup** (lentils simmered with zucchini, celery, onions, potatoes, and spices)
Entrees	✓ **Shish kebab** (chunks of beef, lamb, or chicken marinated and spiced, skewered with tomatoes, onions, and peppers and grilled)
	Mousaka (layers of eggplant, ground lamb, and cheese topped with bechamel sauce)
	Spanikopita (spinach and cheese pie made with phyllo dough)
	✓ **Kibbeh,** baked (cracked wheat mixed with spicy ground meat and stuffed with sauteed onions and pine nuts)
	✓ **Gyros** (combination of seared, spicy lamb and beef, served with lettuce, tomato, onions, and tzateki sauce)

✔ **Sheik el Mahshi** (baked eggplant, stuffed with ground lamb, pine nuts, onions, Middle Eastern spices, and tomato sauce)

✔ **Souvlaki** (marinated and grilled meat, served with lettuce, tomato, onions, and tzateki sauce)

Pasticchio (baked macaroni with ground beef and eggs, topped with a creamy sauce)

✔ **Dolma** (stuffed grape leaves, with ground lamb, rice, onions, and spices)

Falafel (fava beans and chick peas blended with spices and served with tahini or tarator sauce)

✔ **Lah me june** (Armenian pizza, topped with ground meat, parsley, tomatoes, onions, and spices)

✔ **Kafta** (beef ground with parsley, onions, and other spices and served grilled)

✔ **Couscous** (a wheat grain steamed on top of a spicy lamb and vegetable stew)

Side Dishes

✔ **Tabooli** (bulghur salad with raw vegetables)

✔ **Rice pilaf** (long-grain rice seasoned with butter and saffron)

Feta cheese

Kalamata (olives)

✔ **Pita bread**

Desserts	**Baklava** (pastry made with layers of phyllo dough, nuts, and sugar)
	Kataif (pastry made with shredded dough, nuts, and sugar)
	Rice pudding
	✓ **Turkish coffee**
	✓ **American coffee**

May I Take Your Order

Low-Calorie Sample Meal	**Tabooli salad**
	Quantity: ¾ cup
	Exchanges: 1 fat; ½ vegetable; 1 starch
	Gyros plate
	Quantity: 3 oz.
	Exchanges: 3 meat (med.); 1 vegetable
	Pita bread
	Quantity: ¾ pita
	Exchanges: 2 starch
	Low-calorie carbonated beverage
	Quantity: unlimited
	Exchanges: free
Nutrition Summary	560 calories
	32% calories as fat
	26% calories as protein
	42% calories as carbohydrate
	76 mg cholesterol
	1000 mg sodium
Moderate-Calorie Sample Meal	**Fattoush** (dressing on the side)
	Quantity: 1½ cups
	Exchanges: 2 vegetable; ½ starch

Dressing (on the side)
Quantity: 1 tablespoon
Exchanges: 1 fat
Sheik el Mahshi (split order)
Quantity: 1½ cups
Exchanges: 1 meat (med); 1 fat; 2
vegetable
Kibbeh, baked (split order)
Quantity: 1 cup
Exchanges: 1 meat (med); 1
vegetable; 1 starch
Rice pilaf
Quantity: ⅔ cup
Exchanges: 1 fat; 2 starch
Retsina wine
Quantity: 6 oz.
Exchanges: alcohol exchanges not
accounted for

**Nutrition
Summary**

826	calories
33%	calories as fat
15%	calories as protein
38%	calories as carbohydrate
14%	calories as alcohol
50	mg cholesterol
1110	mg sodium

10.

Healthier eating out

French/ Continental Style

Today, continental restaurants offer a wider gamut of choices than ever before. Ingredients and resulting dishes are of multiple ethnic origins and represent a variety of styles and healthiness. In most big cities you still find classic French restaurants that prepare food in the old methods of *haute cuisine.* They serve the familiar rich sauces—béchamel, bernaise, and mornay. But as we entered the 1980s, more and more upper-crust restaurants began to serve the newer French cuisine, labeled nouvelle cuisine. This is a lighter and healthier French cooking style. Today, continental cookery includes foods from all over the world. For instance, the uniqueness of Southeast Asian cookery has influenced dishes served both in American and French restaurants. All of these unique qualities have blended into the "melting pot" of foods available today in America's continental restaurants.

There's definitely a wave toward healthier eating. The newer cooking methods—grilling, stir-frying, blackening, poaching—avoid the fat from butter, eggs, and cream previously used in large volume in haute cuisine. The newer preparation methods and the use of healthier ingredients illustrate how we can enjoy great foods while encouraging lower-fat, calorie-conscious dining.

Southwest regional cookery is catching on with its offerings of black bean soup, blue corn polenta, smoked tomatoes, chipotle, and cilantro sauces. Even Italian cuisine has changed over the last ten years. It's lighter, with more pesto sauces and primavera entrees. There's also Cajun food being served.

So, all in all, continental dining in America is no longer defined by classic French cuisine. There's a wide variety of restaurant choices as well as a wide selection within the menu listings. And the many healthier dishes make "eating continental" more desirable than ever.

THE MENU PROFILE

Continental restaurants are where you go to "dine." No matter what type of food it is—French, Italian, or Southwestern—you have different expectations in a continental restaurant than when you buzz into a fast food spot to grab a quick hamburger. In these restaurants you expect to be "waited on," you expect "white glove" service.

Visits to continental restaurants are often reserved for special occasions—celebrating a birthday, anniversary, or graduation—or important business meals. Unlike the quick order-and-bring-me-a-check restaurants, you expect to linger over your meal, enjoying the food and the relaxing environment. It's common to order alcoholic beverages, be it a mixed drink before eating or wine with dinner. You

might be more likely to top off the dinner with a
cordial or Irish coffee.

All of these factors—the length of time spent
around food, dangerous foods lying around on the
table, the quantity served, more elaborate preparation, higher-fat foods, alcohol, and tempting desserts—can make continental dining more difficult.
Certainly, being successful might take more persis-
tence and just plain "white knuckling" it.

Green Flag Words
- balsamic vinegar or vinaigrette
- cilantro
- roasted red peppers
- sun-dried tomatoes
- blackened
- Cajun spiced
- wine sauce, red or white (make sure no cream is added)
- sauce of tomato, garlic, and spices
- wine and herbs
- green spices—rosemary, tarragon, basil, oregano
- fruit sauces—mango, raspberry, orange, apple
- roasted, steamed, poached
- grilled, marinated, broiled
- en brochette
- mustard sauce (make sure it's not a mustard cream sauce)
- salsa
- available as appetizer portion
- half portions available
- petite or queen size

Red Flag Words
- cheese sauce, cream sauce
- blended with melted cheese
- au gratin
- served with drawn butter

- stuffed with seasoned breadcrumbs
- stuffed and baked with butter sauce
- orange, herb, or shallot butter
- casserole (usually indicates added fat)
- bacon, sausage
- blue cheese
- wrapped in phyllo dough
- wrapped in pastry shell
- hollandaise, mayonnaise
- sour cream, crème fraîche

Special Requests French/Continental Style

- Could you serve the sauce on the side?
- Would you serve the salad dressing on the side?
- Could I get some vinegar or lemon wedges for my salad rather than the dressing?
- May I have some Dijon mustard for my potato?
- Please don't add butter or sour cream to my potato, but bring it on the side.
- Could I ask you how this is prepared?
- Is it possible to have these vegetables steamed rather than sauteed?
- Please bring my appetizer when you bring the others their main course.
- Could we get an extra plate to split this appetizer (or entree)?

- Can you bring several extra forks? We are going to split this dessert.
- May I have this wrapped up to take home?

Typical Menu: *French/Continental Style*

Appetizers

Mussels au gratin (mussels in garlic butter sauce with cheese topping)

✓ **Shrimp,** 4 ozs., marinated and grilled

Stuffed mushrooms (prepared with herbs and seasoned breadcrumbs, topped with rosemary in cream sauce)

Pâté de la maison (pâté de foie gras, served with toast points)

Escargots (snails served with garlic, herbs, butter sauce)

✓ **Vegetable melange** with mustard sauce (freshly cut raw vegetables served in a lettuce cup with curry mustard sauce)

✓ **Grilled asparagus** with lemon soy sauce

Artichoke hearts with feta cheese (artichoke hearts marinated and sauteed in olive oil, topped with crumbled feta cheese)

✓ indicates
preferred choices

Soups	**Soup du jour** (server will describe today's special)
	French onion soup (traditional style, served in a crock with melted cheese)
	✓ **Jellied consomme** (clear light broth, served chilled)
	✓ **Gazpacho** (cold tomato-based soup of assorted pureed fresh vegetables)
Salads	✓ **House salad** (mixture of romaine and Bibb lettuce, with red onions, red peppers, and sprouts, with raspberry vinaigrette dressing)
	✓ **Exotic greens** (mixture of radicchio, endive, watercress, and jicama, with balsamic vinaigrette)
	✓ **Spinach salad** (fresh spinach, topped with sliced mushrooms, egg, and bacon bits, with hot bacon dressing)
Meat Entrees*	**Beef Wellington** (fillet of beef covered with thin layer of goose liver pâté and wrapped in flaky pastry shell, topped with Bordelaise sauce)
	✓ **Petite filet mignon** (6 oz.) with mushroom sauce
	New York sirloin broiled steak, 12 ozs.
	✓ **Marinated pork chop,** 10 ozs. (broiled in sherry and lemon herb sauce)
	✓ **Rack of lamb** (broiled with a glaze of honey mustard sauce)

Veal Oscar (veal cutlet sauteed with lobster meat and asparagus, topped with hollandaise sauce)

Poultry Entrees*

Chicken Kiev (boneless breast of chicken, filled with herb butter and cheese garlic, topped with butter sauce)

✓ **Chicken saute** (sliced chicken breast, sauteed with sun-dried tomatoes, asparagus, and herbs in olive oil)

Duck à l'orange (one-half Long Island duckling grilled and basted with orange glaze)

✓ **Duck with raspberry sauce** (sliced breast of duck served with light raspberry lemon sauce)

Seafood Entrees*

Stuffed shrimp (four jumbo shrimp, stuffed with blend of crabmeat and seasoned breadcrumbs, baked and basted with garlic butter sauce)

✓ **Poached salmon** with smoked tomato sauce and cilantro

Dover sole in champagne cream sauce

✓ **Blackened tuna** served with mango chutney sauce

Other Entrees*

Seafood fettucini (shrimp and scallops, topped with basil cream sauce)

Cheese-stuffed tortellini topped with sauteed broccoli and mushrooms

✓ **Oriental stir-fry** (fresh garden
vegetables, stir-fried in olive oil,
tamari, garlic, and lemon, served
over brown rice)

*Entrees served with choice of
rice pilaf, baked potato, steamed
red bliss potatoes, or fried potato
puffs*

Vegetables

✓ **Squash and zucchini,** sauteed in
lemon herb butter
✓ **Snow peas,** sauteed with red
pepper
Creamed spinach
✓ **Asparagus,** steamed and topped
with hollandaise sauce

Desserts

✓ **Strawberries** topped with crème
fraîche
Key lime pie
Peanut butter cheesecake
Chocolate raspberry cake
(double fudge cake, iced and
filled with raspberry jam)
✓ **Fresh raspberries** topped with
Chambord liqueur

May I Take Your Order

Low-Calorie Sample Meal	**Shrimp,** marinated and grilled (listed as appetizer but request as main course) *Quantity:* 4 ozs. *Exchanges:* 3 meat (lean); 1 fat **Exotic greens** (dressing on the side) *Quantity:* 1–2 cups *Exchanges:* 1–2 vegetable **Balsamic vinaigrette dressing** (on the side) *Quantity:* 1 tablespoon *Exchanges:* 1 fat **Red bliss potatoes,** steamed (request no butter) *Quantity:* 2 *Exchanges:* 2 starch **Strawberries** (hold crème fraiche) *Quantity:* ½ cup *Exchanges:* 1 fruit **Wine** *Quantity:* 6 ozs. *Exchanges:* account for calories but don't omit exchanges
Nutrition Summary	581 calories 20% calories as fat 23% calories as protein 40% calories as carbohydrate 17% calories as alcohol 166 mg cholesterol 650 mg sodium

Moderate-Calorie Sample Meal

House salad (dressing on the side)
Quantity: 1–2 cups
Exchanges: 1–2 vegetables
Raspberry vinaigrette dressing (on the side)
Quantity: 2 tablespoons
Exchanges: 2 fat
Petite filet mignon
Quantity: 3 ozs. (½ order)
Exchanges: 3 meat (med.)
Red bliss potatoes, steamed (request no butter)
Quantity: 1 medium
Exchanges: 1 starch
Oriental stir-fry with brown rice
Quantity: ½ order
Exchanges: 2 fat; 2 vegetable; 2 starch
Fresh raspberries with Chambord
Quantity: ½ cup
Exchanges: 1 fruit; alcohol exchanges not accounted for

Nutrition Summary

 858 calories
 32% calories as fat
 18% calories as protein
 44% calories as carbohydrate
  6% calories as alcohol
  67 mg cholesterol
790 mg sodium

Healthier eating out
Seafood Style

Seafood, from fin fish to shellfish, is served in a wide range of restaurants and prepared in a multitude of ways from healthy to decadently high in fat. Consider for a second the difference between grilled swordfish and lobster Newburg.

The message is loud and clear—eat more seafood: it is good for you. Indeed, the benefits of eating healthfully prepared seafood, once thought to be "brain food," are now confirmed. And many Americans, knowing that fish is good for the heart as well as the waistline, are eating more seafood than ever.

Due to this increased demand for healthfully prepared fin fish and shellfish, many new and tasty cooking methods are evolving. Methods of grilling on mesquite chips and the Cajun preparation of blackening have come into vogue. Mustard sauces, simple lemon or wine sauces, garlic, and roasted pepper or spicy tomato salsa are all finding favor among the health conscious.

THE MENU PROFILE

All seafood, prior to preparation, is among the healthiest protein food available. Many health characteristics of fish are destroyed quickly if it is prepared in a high-fat and calorie recipe. Consider the nutritional differences between a boiled lobster and a baked, stuffed lobster served with drawn butter or, worse yet, lobster Newburg or pie. You start off with the same lobster but change the end product substantially with high-fat ingredients.

All seafood, prior to preparation, ranges from about 30–60 calories per cooked ounce. Cod, scallops, and monkfish are on the low-calorie side, whereas swordfish, salmon, and blue fish are on the higher-calorie side due to their slightly high fat content. Still, all are low in calories and fat compared to red meats. Even extra-lean ground beef usually rings in at about 75 calories per ounce cooked.

With the emphasis today on lowering fat, saturated fat, and cholesterol intake, fish is a food of choice. However, unknown to many, there is little difference in dietary cholesterol between meats and seafood. Yet, fin fish and shellfish are relatively low in saturated fat.

In addition to their health and calorie-counting benefits, in recent years some fish, including salmon, bluefish, mackerel, sardines, rainbow trout, and eel, have been found to contain omega-3 fats. These are polyunsaturated fats that are suspected to boost heart health. However, the verdict is still pending on the benefits of omega-3 fats.

Fish has an additional health benefit in its low sodium content. Most fresh fin fish and shellfish are low in sodium compared to other protein foods: meat, cheese, and poultry. You will find that a few items, such as surimi, crab, lobster, shrimp, mussels, and oysters have slightly higher sodium count. Refer to the chart for sodium nutrition information.

But, don't think you can eat fish with impunity. Most fast-food preparation destroys anything healthy about fish by breading, frying, and baking in sauces. But some fast-food seafood chains have introduced baked and broiled items. Try new varieties of seafood, such as the increasingly popular mahi mahi (dolphin fish, no relation to the sea mammal), monkfish, and mussels. Be adventurous and try the many new and creative low-fat and low-calorie preparation methods used today. Consider poached salmon, steamed halibut and vegetables, barbecued shrimp, mesquite-grilled tuna, swordfish kabobs, and blackened bluefish just for starters.

Green Flag Words	• broiled; barbecued; steamed
	• stir-fried; teriyaki
	• blackened; Cajun style
	• sauteed in light wine sauce
	• mesquite-grilled; grilled
	• in spicy tomato sauce; in marinara sauce
	• with herbs, spices, lemon, garlic
	• marinated
	• kabobs
	• served with gazpacho salsa

Red Flag Words	• fried; deep-fried
	• breaded and fried; batter-dipped and fried
	• fish 'n chips
	• creamy; served in creamy wine sauce
	• served with cheese sauce
	• en casserole
	• lobster or seafood pie
	• Newburg; Thermidor
	• baked stuffed; stuffed and rolled
	• creamy chowder or bisque

**Special Requests
Seafood Style**

- Please broil dry with a few breadcrumbs.
- Bring me a few extra lemon wedges.
- Please serve the salad with dressing on the side.
- Do you have balsamic vinegar I could use on my salad?
- Could I substitute a baked potato for French fries?
- Could I substitute a dinner salad for the creamy cole slaw?
- Please bring the butter and sour cream on the side.
- Could I get a doggie bag at the beginning of my meal?
- Please bring an extra plate; we are gong to share.
- Please bring my appetizer as my main course, but I'll have my salad with the others.

Typical Menu: Seafood Style

Raw Bar	✔ **Oysters** on the halfshell
	✔ **Cherrystone clams** on the halfshell
	✔ **Assorted sashimi** with white rice
Appetizers	**Baked clams Casino**
	✔ **Steamed clams**
	Cajun-fried calamari with spicy tomato sauce
✔ indicates preferred choices	✔ **Marinated calamari**
	Oysters Rockefeller

✔ **Barbecued shrimp**
Scallops tempura
✔ **Shrimp cocktail**—6 large shrimp
with cocktail sauce

Soups

✔ **Shrimp gumbo**
✔ **Fish chowder**
New England clam chowder
✔ **Manhattan clam chowder**
Lobster bisque

Fin Fish Entrees* ✔ **Broiled mackerel** with light
mustard and dill sauce
Baked stuffed sole
Scrod, stuffed and baked, in
cheese sauce
✔ **Swordfish kabobs** with peppers,
mushrooms, and red onions

The following fish are available
broiled, steamed with vegetables,
mesquite-grilled, blackened, or
grilled with teriyaki sauce:
✔ **Bluefish**   ✔ **Haddock**
✔ **Halibut**   ✔ **Mahi mahi** (dolphin
fish)   ✔ **Monkfish**   ✔ **Redfish**
✔ **Salmon**   ✔ **Swordfish**
The following fish are available
fried or Cajun-fried:
Bass   **Catfish**   **Flounder**
Haddock

Shellfish Entrees* ✔ **Baked stuffed jumbo shrimp**
✔ **Boiled Maine lobster** with drawn
butter and lemon, served with
corn on the cob, creamy coleslaw,
and watermelon

Lobster pie (lobster meat in
cream sauce casserole, topped
with breadcrumbs)

✓ **Scallops** sauteed in spicy tomato
sauce

✓ **Alaskan king crab** claws steamed
and served with drawn butter

Seafood casserole (crabmeat,
shrimp, scallops, and others
combined with Parmesan cheese
cream sauce and topped with
breadcrumbs)

✓ **Cioppino** (clams, shrimp, lobster,
and calamari braised in tomato
sauce and served over pasta)

✓ **Bouillabaisse** (seafood stew with
monkfish, cod, and lobster)

*Note: All entrees are served with
a choice of two of the following
items:

French fries   ✓ **Baked potato**
   ✓ **Saffron rice**   ✓ **Rice pilaf**
   ✓ **Tossed green salad**

Creamy coleslaw
   ✓ **Sauteed zucchini,** yellow
      squash, and onion
   ✓ **Steamed fresh broccoli**

Desserts   **New York cheesecake**
✓ **Fresh strawberries** or
raspberries with crème de cassis
and whipped cream

✓ **Watermelon**
Chocolate layer cake
Apple pie à la mode with vanilla
ice cream

May I Take Your Order

Low-Calorie Sample Meal	**Tossed green salad** (dressing on the side) *Quantity:* 2 cups *Exchanges:* 2 vegetables **Vinaigrette,** lemon-basil dressing *Quantity:* 1 tablespoon *Exchanges:* 1 fat **Sauteed scallops** in spicy tomato sauce *Quantity:* 1½ cups *Exchanges:* 3 meat (lean); 1 vegetable **Saffron rice** *Quantity:* ⅔ cup *Exchanges:* 2 starch **Broccoli,** steamed fresh (hold butter) *Quantity:* ½ cup *Exchanges:* 1 vegetable
Nutrition Summary	540 calories 31% calories as fat 31% calories as protein 38% calories as carbohydrate 60 mg cholesterol 1100 mg sodium
Moderate-Calorie Sample Meal	**Fish chowder** *Quantity:* ½ cup *Exchanges:* ½ milk; 1 meat (lean) **Steamed clams** with lemon and clam broth *Quantity:* 10–15 clams *Exchanges:* 2 meats (lean)

Boiled Maine lobster with drawn
butter and lemon (hold butter)
Quantity: 1½-lb. lobster
Exchanges: 3 meats (lean)
Corn on the cob (hold butter and
salt)
Quantity: 2 ears
Exchanges: 3 starch
Watermelon
Quantity: 2 cups
Exchanges: 2 fruits

Nutrition Summary   715 calories
31% calories as fat
29% calories as protein
41% calories as carbohydrate
165 mg cholesterol
1350 mg sodium

12.

Healthier eating out
American Style

At mid-priced "American food" restaurants serving "American fare," your order may be a mushroom cheeseburger with French fries, a chef's salad in a fried tortilla shell, or a teriyaki chicken breast sandwich. These restaurants might be defined as a few steps up from fast food and a few steps down from continental.

Though we call these "American-style" restaurants, what really is American fare? The menus generally reflect a melting pot of multiple cuisines. American fare is ultimately a blending of foods from different cultures with American adaptations. On the menus you'll find echoes of multiple ethnic cuisines, especially the popular Mexican, Italian, and Oriental.

Selections on these menus are hardly ideal when viewed in terms of healthy eating goals. Fried mozzarella sticks, quiche Lorraine, fried shrimp tempura, or a Philadelphia cheese steak are just a sampling of the usual high-fat, high-calorie offerings. But by no means should these restaurants be avoided. There are good choices, and where there's a will, there's a way.

We've got a long way to go before these menus list a wealth of healthy selections. It will be great when we see healthier appetizers, half or smaller portions available at lower prices, and more low-fat or no-oil salad dressings. But for the next few years at least, you'll have to maneuver your way through the mine field of high-fat and high-calorie menu listings when eating American fare.

Green Flag Words

- sauteed onions, peppers, mushrooms, jalapeños
- BBQ sauce (watch sugar content)
- cocktail sauce
- teriyaki sauce; Cajun sauce
- honey mustard (watch sugar content)
- mustard (Dijon, Pommery)
- crisp lettuce and/or sliced tomatoes
- green or red onions
- spicy Mexican beef or chicken
- blackened; mesquite-grilled
- with oriental sauce
- marinated and broiled
- charbroiled; barbecued; stir-fry
- low-calorie salad dressing

Red Flag Words

- cheese (grated, melted, topped with, smothered in)
- guacamole
- bacon (strips, crisp, crumbled); sausage
- golden fried
- crispy, deep-fried
- battered and fried
- rolled in breadcrumbs and fried

- sour cream
- with cheese, bacon, and/or sour cream
- blue cheese (crumbled, topped with, salad dressing)
- creamy garlic butter
- crisp tortilla shell; nachos
- large, jumbo, piled high, stacked
- Alfredo sauce; cream sauce
- mayonnaise, garlic mayonnaise

Special Requests American Style

- On the blackened chicken sandwich, please leave off the cheese.
- On the roast beef sandwich, can you make sure they don't put any butter or mayonnaise on the bread? However, I'd like a side of mustard or horseradish.
- Do you have Mexican hot sauce? Could I get a bit to use on my salad?
- Please hold the sour cream, but you can load on the lettuce and tomato.
- Please bring me a little bowl of low-calorie dressing that I can use for the vegetable dip.
- Could I substitute a baked potato for the French fries?
- Could you leave the fries off the plate?
- Could I get that sandwich on whole-wheat bread rather than a croissant?
- We are going to split the salad and the hamburger, so please bring an extra plate.

Typical Menu: American Style

Appetizers

Nachos (nacho chips covered with melted cheese, jalapeño peppers, and hot sauce)

Buffalo chicken wings (marinated chicken wings in hot and spicy sauce, lightly fried, and served with blue cheese dressing)

✓ **Peel-and-eat shrimp** (¼ lb. boiled shrimp with cocktail sauce)

Potato skins (fried potato skins, filled with cheese and choice of bacon bits, sour cream, and/or onions)

Mozzarella sticks (mozzarella cheese, rolled in breadcrumbs and fried; served with marinara sauce)

✓ **Raw bar platter** (oysters on the halfshell, steamed clams, and jumbo shrimp, served with cocktail sauce)

Soups

New England clam chowder (creamy chowder with clams and potato, served with oyster crackers)

French onion soup (smothered with Swiss cheese)

✓ indicates   ✓ **Chili** (spicy mixture of pinto
preferred choices   beans, ground beef, and sauteed

onions and peppers, topped with
onions and Monterey Jack cheese)
✓ **Vegetable gumbo** (blend of
garden vegetables, onions,
tomatoes, broccoli, and green
beans simmered in Cajun spices)

Salads
✓ **House salad** (blend of greens,
with sliced cucumbers and
tomatoes, topped with alfalfa
sprouts; choice of dressings)
✓ **Seafood pasta salad** (rotini
blended with baby shrimp and
red pepper, tossed with Italian
dressing, and served on bed of
mixed greens)
✓ **Blackened chicken salad** (slices
of marinated and blackened
chicken breast, with mixed salad
greens, avocado slices, cherry
tomatoes, and broccoli, topped
with shredded Swiss cheese and
croutons)
✓ **Chef salad** (julienne sliced
turkey, ham, and Swiss cheese,
served on bed of lettuce, diced
tomatoes, red and green pepper
rounds, all in crispy tortilla shell)
Choice of Salad Dressings:
House (creamy garlic)
✓ Italian   French   Blue cheese
Thousand Island   Hot bacon
✓ Lemon vinaigrette
✓ Oil and vinegar
✓ Low-calorie Italian   Ranch

Sandwiches	All sandwiches served with French fries and creamy coleslaw

✔ **French dip** (thinly sliced beef, topped with melted provolone cheese, and served with natural gravy)

✔ **Blackened chicken sandwich** (breast of chicken marinated and blackened on the grill, topped with lettuce, tomato, sprouts, crisp bacon slices, and Cheddar cheese)

Tuna melt (creamy tuna salad, topped with melted Swiss cheese)

Seafood salad croissant (flaky croissant filled with mixture of creamy seafood salad, celery, and onions)

Burgers   All burgers served with sliced tomato on bed of lettuce, with French fries and side of creamy coleslaw

Regular hamburgers are 6 ozs. of ground beef and jumbo are 9 ozs.

✔ **American hamburger**

Cheeseburger (add slice of Swiss or Cheddar cheese)

Bacon cheeseburger (add several slices of bacon and slice of Monterey Jack cheese)

✔ **Veggie burger** (add sauteed onions, peppers, and mushrooms)

Chili burger (add spicy Mexican chili)

Hot Entrees	✓ **Fajitas** (choice of chicken or beef, grilled with sliced onions and green peppers, served with warm flour tortillas and sides of sour cream, guacamole, Mexican hot sauce)
	Baby back ribs (robust portion with fried onion rings and baked beans)
	✓ **Teriyaki chicken breast** (served with rice pilaf and sauteed vegetables)
	Chicken fried steak (sirloin steak, dipped in batter, and fried; served with country gravy, baked potato, and steamed vegetables)
	✓ **Oriental stir-fry** (choice of chicken, shrimp, or just vegetables; served over Chinese egg noodles)
Combinations	✓ **Soup and salad** (bowl of any soup and house salad)
	Quiche and salad (slice of ham, broccoli, and mushroom quiche, served with house salad)
	✓ **Soup or Salad and half sandwich** (soup or house salad with half of French dip or seafood salad sandwich)
Side Orders	**French fries**
	Creamy coleslaw
	✓ **Rice pilaf**
	✓ **Baked potato** with butter and/or sour cream
	✓ **Sauteed vegetables**

Desserts

   ✔ **Deep-dish apple pie** à la mode (vanilla ice cream)

   New York cheesecake (topped with choice of strawberry or blueberry sauce)

   Ice cream (two scoops of vanilla, chocolate, or strawberry)

   Hot fudge sundae

   ✔ **Sorbet** (two scoops of raspberry or lemon sherbet)

MAY I TAKE YOUR ORDER

Low-Calorie Sample Meal

Peel-and-eat shrimp
Quantity: 1 order (9–12 med.)
Exchanges: 3 meat (lean)

Cocktail sauce for above
Quantity: 2 tablespoons
Exchanges: free

Oriental stir-fry, vegetable
Quantity: 1½ cups
Exchanges: 2 fat; 3 vegetable

Chinese egg noodles with above
Quantity: 1 cup
Exchanges: 2 starch

Sorbet, raspberry (split order)
Quantity: ¾ cup
Exchanges: ½ fat; 1 starch; 1 fruit

Mineral water
Quantity: unlimited
Exchanges: free

Nutrition Summary	608 calories
	21% calories as fat
	21% calories as protein
	58% calories as carbohydrate
	227 mg cholesterol (high, due to shrimp)
	970 mg sodium

Moderate-Calorie Sample Meal	**House salad** (dressing on the side)
	Quantity: 2 cups
	Exchanges: 2 vegetable
	Blue cheese dressing (request vinegar)
	Quantity: 1 tablespoon
	Exchanges: 1 fat
	Teriyaki chicken breast
	Quantity: 4 oz.
	Exchanges: 4 meat (lean)
	Rice pilaf
	Quantity: 1 cup
	Exchanges: 3 starch
	Sauteed vegetables
	Quantity: 1 cup
	Exchanges: 1 fat; 2 vegetable
	Wine
	Quantity: 1 glass (6 oz.)
	Exchanges: alcohol exchanges not accounted for

Nutrition Summary	758 calories
	31% calories as fat
	22% calories as protein
	32% calories as carbohydrate
	15% calories as alcohol
	120 mg cholesterol
	1170 mg sodium

13.

Healthier eating out
Fast-Food Style

Until recently the use of the words fast food and
healthy in the same breath was an oxymoron. Not
any more! The menu offerings of frozen yogurt, chef
salad, and grilled chicken sandwich are now regulars
on fast-food menus of the '90s. Fast-food restaurants
continue to feed millions of mouths daily, literally all
over the world.

In the 1980s, the fast food business was stimu-
lated by our "quicker the better" mentality. Today,
the chains have all jumped, in fact played leapfrog
with each other, to be first on the healthy, fast-food
bandwagon. There are now more healthy options
than ever before and due to the industry's fierce
competition, more on the way. You can also expect
that fast-food chains will continue promoting the
healthiness of their foods for some time to come.
However, take these claims with a grain of salt—no,
maybe pepper instead.

The largest percentage of fast-food selections continue to be fat-drenched disasters, from a fried fish sandwich with a dollop of tartar sauce to a double bacon cheeseburger with special sauce. But fast-food menus have and will continue to expand in the ever-competitive market. Think back to the old days when fast-food menus were simply burgers, fries, and soda. Now it's not unusual to hear about chains experimenting with pizza, lobster rolls, chicken enchiladas, and who knows what's next. These restaurants can hardly be classified as burger joints anymore.

Reviewed here are the commonly ordered foods from major national chains serving hamburgers, chicken, and assorted other goodies. Many other fast foods are discussed in the chapters on brunch, lunch, pizza, and salad bars. The table later in this chapter provides a representative sampling of nutrition data.

Hamburgers

The race is now on to introduce leaner hamburgers to the menu. McDonald's led the pack with their McLean. Hardee's Lean Deluxe was next to follow suit. Others will likely appear in due time. Though lean burgers are a healthier choice, once special sauce or a slice of cheese are added, the result is no low-fat wonder.

Remember, as the size of the hamburger and number of patties increase, so do the calories and fat. Small hamburgers contain around two ounces of protein, the quarter-pounders have about three, and the doubles and triples have upward of four ounces. That's not counting the frequently added cheese. Healthwise, you are better off if you have to ask the famous question, "Where's the beef?" If you're left searching for the beef, you're likely eating less saturated fat and cholesterol.

As the number of added ingredients mount, so does fat and calories. The frequent additions of cheese, special sauces, (usually mayonnaise-based), and bacon add fat and calories. Whereas pickles, onions, lettuce, tomatoes, mustard, and catsup increase the flavor without the fat. Compare the difference between a plain hamburger at Burger King, with 270 calories and 36% fat, to their bacon double cheeseburger, with 515 calories and 54% fat. If you've got the calories to spare, order two simple burgers rather than one that's loaded.

Roast Beef Sandwiches

Several chains have made their name with roast beef sandwiches, and others have added these to their growing list of menu items. Generally, the regular or junior sandwich without added cheese is in the vicinity of our 30% fat goal and might be a better choice than a hamburger for improved nutrition.

As with the burgers, avoid the high-fat extras—cheese, special sauces, and so on. But go ahead and use the spicy barbecue sauces for extra punch. Arby's introduced their light menu in mid-1991, and their Light Roast Beef Deluxe rings in at about 31% fat and a reasonable 300 calories.

Chicken Sandwiches

It used to be that fried chicken was the only choice in fast-food spots, but times have changed. Burger King leapfrogged ahead on this one, and today most chains include a grilled chicken sandwich in their repertory. Generally, they are a healthier choice than a loaded hamburger or a fried-chicken sandwich or the fried chicken pieces. But don't be fooled by the healthy sounding words, "grilled" and "chicken"; some of the sandwiches sport heavy sauces, and it drives the fat calories right up to over 40% and higher.

Hardee's and Arby's chicken sandwiches and Jack in the Box's Chicken Fajita Pita, to name a few, are good choices. Hardee's has also added a light roast turkey sandwich that uses a low-fat sauce and keeps the fat calories below a new low of 20%

Chicken Pieces

These nutritional wonders were first introduced by McDonald's and are now stocked by many other chains. No matter whose version, these are battered and fried, with the result equaling a large dose of fat. Loaded with around 50% fat, there are just too many healthier options today to even think of eating chicken chunks.

Fried Chicken

A few chains specialize in serving fried chicken to the masses. Kentucky Fried Chicken, or KFC, as they now want to be called to avoid the "F" word, is the leader in the field. There's little nutritionally redeeming in these eateries. KFC recently introduced Skinfree Crispy chicken. Although, as the name implies, it is skin-free, the calories and fat are not far different from the Original recipe.

If you eat fried chicken once in a blue moon, set a limit of one piece. Complement it with mashed potatoes or corn on the cob rather than more fried offerings.

Fried Fish Sandwiches

Fish, you say, is healthy, of course. Wrong. In this case the fish gets lost among the batter, oil, tartar sauce, and maybe a slice of cheese. Possibly close to the worst choice on a fast-food menu is the fried fish sandwich. Without counting the French fries, these run upward of 500 calories, 50% from fat.

Steer clear is the best advice. If you find a baked, broiled, or grilled fish sandwich eventually showing up on menus in fast-food fish stops, it might be a reasonable choice.

French Fries

A fast-food order without French fries? It used to be a sacrilege. Now there are alternative accessories—

baked potato or side salad. But French fries are sometimes just a must. And considered on their own, French fries, that is, a regular order, don't deserve the criticism they've received. The sodium content is low, there's no cholesterol, and potatoes do offer great nutrition.

The problem with fries is that they accompany an already high-fat meal. When ordering fries, order a regular-size portion, or split them with your fast-food pal.

Baked Potatoes

Baked potatoes have been a healthier alternative on several fast-food menus for a while now. Once again, we start off with one of the best nutritional bets, a potato, but we find a multitude of ways to drive up the fat with butter, margarine, cheese, bacon, sour cream, chili, or a combo. The best of the toppings, though none are wonderful, are broccoli and cheese or chili and cheese. The best bet is the great-tasting baked potato solo, with some salt and pepper.

Salads

Side, garden, chef, and more, salads have been a welcome addition to the fast-food menu, and they're available in just about every spot. Most restaurants go with the pre-packaged salad, though a few salad bars are left in fast-food spots. The side or garden salads improve the healthiness of most fast-food meals as long as care is taken to use a minimal amount of the ridiculously large serving of dressing provided.

The salads that constitute a meal—chef, chicken, taco, and others—range from low-calorie great choices to healthy-sounding delusions. They range from a low 100 calories for the chicken salad to over 500 for others. So don't be fooled by that healthy-sounding word, "salad."

The biggest problem is the dressing. The regular portion, be it blue cheese, Thousand Island, or others, packs on another 100 or so fat calories. Dressings also drastically raise the sodium level. Reduce your calorie intake by using a small amount of dressing and taking advantage of the light varieties.

Beverages

By far, one of the best beverage picks is low-fat or skim milk. Fruit juice is often available but not very appealing with a sandwich. Be careful not to order a sugar-loaded fruit drink thinking it is juice.

For non-caloric beverages, you can choose from low-calorie soda, hot or iced coffee, or tea. It's best to avoid the shakes. They add a few hundred calories and quite a dose of fat. Further information of beverages is given in another chapter.

May I Take Your Order

Low-Calorie Sample Meal	**Baked potato** with chili and cheese *Quantity:* 1 *Exchanges:* 1½ meat (med.); 2 fat; 4 starch **Low-calorie carbonated beverage** *Quantity:* unlimited *Exchanges:* free
Nutrition Summary	481 calories 35% calories as fat 19% calories as protein 46% calories as carbohydrate 31 mg cholesterol 701 mg sodium

Low-Calorie Sample Meal	**Grilled chicken sandwich** with condiments *Quantity:* 1 *Exchanges:* 2 meat (lean); 2 starch **Garden salad** *Quantity:* regular size *Exchanges:* 2 vegetable **Reduced-calorie Italian dressing** *Quantity:* 2 tablespoons *Exchanges:* 1 fat **Low-fat milk** *Quantity:* 8 oz. *Exchanges:* 1 milk
Nutrition Summary	493 calories 25% calories as fat 28% calories as protein 47% calories as carbohydrate 48 mg cholesterol 1180 mg sodium
Moderate-Calorie Sample Meal	**Lean hamburger** without cheese *Quantity:* 1 *Exchanges:* 3 meat (lean); 2 starch; 1 fat **French fries** *Quantity:* small order *Exchanges:* 2 starch; 2 fat **Side salad** *Quantity:* 1 *Exchanges:* free (without dressing) **Low-calorie carbonated beverage** *Quantity:* medium *Exchanges:* free
Nutrition Summary	590 calories 39% calories as fat 16% calories as protein 45% calories as carbohydrate 80 mg cholesterol 870 mg sodium

Little Changes Add Up to a Big Nutrition Difference

Food Choice	Calories	Fat (gr)	% Cals. as Fat	Sodium (mg)	Cholesterol
CHANGE THIS ORDER:					
Quarter-pound hamburger with cheese and sauces	520	29	50	1150	118
French fries, large	400	22	46	200	16
Cola beverage, regular	140	0	0	15	0
Totals	1060	51	43	1365	134
TO:					
Lean hamburger, no cheese	340	13	34	650	80
Baked potato	250	2	7	60	0
Garden salad	42	0	0	23	0
Italian dressing, reduced-calorie (2 tbsp.)	50	4	70	360	0
Low-calorie beverage, 12 oz.	1	0	0	30	0
Totals	683	19	25	1103	80
CHANGE THIS ORDER:					
Chicken specialty sandwich	685	40	52	1417	53
French fries, large	400	22	46	200	16
Chocolate shake, low fat	320	2	5	240	10
Apple pie	260	15	34	240	0
Totals	1665	79	34	2097	139
TO:					
Grilled chicken sandwich, no cheese	263	6	20	620	39
French fries, small	220	12	48	110	9
Side salad	60	3	50	85	41
Italian dressing, reduced-calorie (1 tbsp.)	25	2	36	185	0
Low-calorie beverage	1	0	0	30	0
Totals	568	23	31	1030	89

Nutrition Information on Selected Fast Foods +

(see Abbreviation Key following table)

Food	Calories	Fat (gr)	Sodium (mg)	Choles- terol(mg)
Lean Hamburgers				
McLean (MD)	310			
Lean deluxe (H)	340	13	650	80
Single Hamburgers				
Hamburger (BK)	272	11	505	37
Cheeseburger (MD)	310	14	750	53
Cheeseburger (H)	320	14	490	20
Single with everything (W)	420	21	890	70
Deluxe Hamburgers				
Quarter-Pounder with cheese (MD)	410	21	660	86
Big deluxe (H)	500	30	760	70
Whopper with cheese (BK)	706	44	1177	115
Roast Beef Sandwich				
Regular Rax (R)	262	10	707	15
Light roast beef deluxe (A)	294	10	826	42
Regular roast beef (A)	353	15	588	39
Beef, bacon 'n cheddar (R)	523	32	1042	42
Grilled Chicken Sandwich				
Light chicken deluxe (A)	263	6	620	39
Chicken fajita pita (JB)	292	8	703	34
Grilled chicken sandwich (W)	340	13	815	60
BK broiler (BK)	379	18	764	53
Fried Chicken Sandwich				
Chicken sandwich (W)	440	19	725	60
McChicken (MD)	490	29	780	43
Chicken specialty (BK)	685	40	1417	82
Chicken Pieces (small order)				
Chicken tenders (BK)	236	13	541	46
Chicken pieces (MD)	270	15	580	56
Sauces				
Barbecue (W)	50	—	100	—
Hot mustard (MD)	70	4	270	5

Food	Calo-ries	Fat (gr)	Sodium (mg)	Choles-terol(mg)
Fried Chicken				
Skinfree Crispy (KFC) center breast	296	16	435	59
Skinfree Crispy (KFC) thigh	256	17	394	68
Original center breast (KFC)	283	15	672	93
Extra crispy breast (KFC)	342	20	790	114
Fried Fish Sandwich				
Fish filet (W)	460	25	780	50
Fisherman fillet (H)	500	24	1030	70
Fish supreme (JB)	510	27	1040	55
French Fries (regular)				
McDonald's	220	12	110	9
Hardee's	230	11	85	—
Rax	282	14	75	3
Baked Potatoes				
Plain (A)	243	2	58	—
Broccoli 'n cheddar (A)	417	18	361	22
Chili 'n cheese (W)	500	18	630	25
Salads (not including dressing)				
Garden (W)	70	2	60	—
Garden (BK)	95	5	125	15
Side (A)	25	—	30	—
Side (MD)	60	3	85	41
Roast chicken salad (A)	180	7	337	45
Chef salad (MD)	230	13	490	128
Taco salad (W)	530	23	825	35
Chicken cashew (A)	590	37	1140	65
Salad Dressing (per packet, or 4 tbsp.)				
Light Italian (A)	23	1	1110	—
Light Italian (W)	50	4	370	—
French (R)	275	22	442	—
Blue cheese (BK)	300	32	512	58
Frozen Yogurt/Milkshake				
Vanilla Cone (MD)	100	1	80	3
Frozen Yogurt (H)	160	4	75	10
Lowfat Milkshake (MD)	320	2	240	10

Abbreviations:

A	Arby's	**KFC**	Kentucky Fried Chicken
BK	Burger King	**MD**	McDonald's
H	Hardee's	**R**	Rax
JB	Jack in the Box	**W**	Wendy's

+All information is supplied by specified restaurant. All information based on nutrient evaluation of September, 1991.

14.

Healthier eating out
Luncheon Style

Surprisingly, lunch is the meal most frequently eaten away from home. The National Restaurant Association adds that over half of consumers eat lunch out at least once a week. It is certainly important, then, to choose your restaurants and luncheon foods carefully.

THE MENU PROFILE

Your lunch order is likely to fall into the same groove as dinner. Unfortunately, the groove people frequently get caught in is a high-fat one. For instance, many people tolerate a tuna salad and bologna sandwich rotation forever. They are simply on automatic pilot when ordering out or carrying lunch from home. The goal is to get the mission of eating lunch accomplished rather than worrying much about what is eaten. Often that sandwich is complemented with a bag of chips, order of French fries, or creamy coleslaw. Unknowingly, a high-fat lunch has been eaten.

Once again, careful attention to foods high in fat is the first consideration when deciding what to order. If you're ordering a sandwich, think about choosing lean items and those not mixed with lots of mayonnaise. Be careful of added accessories— potato chips, French fries, coleslaw, and potato salad are all high-fat items. Think about asking for substitutes or ordering alternative side dishes such as a tossed salad, vinegar-based coleslaw, sliced tomatoes and lettuce, or a big pickle (if you can handle the sodium). If you want a crunchy addition consider grabbing a bag of popcorn or pretzels as lower-fat alternatives. You still get the crunch but lots less fat.

Sandwich Shops—Best Choices

Whatever the aura, food listings are often quite similar from one sandwich spot to the next. There are some great healthy choices on most of these menus. Don't shy away from sandwiches, thinking the bread is loaded with calories. Remember, it's what's between the slices that's the problem. So don't remove the top part of the roll or bread and just eat the insides and the bottom half. You're better off taking out and sharing the meat and eating all the bread.

There are usually various breads from which to choose. Often the listings include white, whole-wheat, light and dark rye, hard rolls, croissants, and Syrian pocket bread. If you can get a 100 percent whole-wheat bread, that's great. The croissant is definitely a choice to avoid; it's loaded with fat. Syrian pocket, or pita bread, as it is often called, is a great choice, especially if you are closely watching calories.

The best sandwich fillers are turkey breast, sliced chicken, grilled chicken breast, roast beef, and ham. If you are on a very low sodium meal plan, ham might not be the right choice, but otherwise, on occasion, it's a fine alternative. Try to avoid or reduce the cheese, often layered on top. You've already got plenty of protein, and you don't need the fat and cholesterol from cheese. Request that the meat be topped with plenty of lettuce and tomato to expand the volume. Be careful to instruct the waitperson or preparer not to add butter, margarine, or mayonnaise to the bread. Think about using mustard, ketchup, or horseradish (if available) to moisten the bread and spice up the sandwich with very few calories and no fat.

Delicatessens —Best Choices

Beef brisket, turkey breast, smoked turkey, lean roast beef—all are fine choices. In many delis you'll find extra-lean corned beef and pastrami. The biggest problem is that the sandwiches are loaded with meat. The bread hardly balances on top of the pile of thinly sliced meat. A great idea for portion control is to have one person order the sandwich and the other request two slices of bread or a roll. Split the portion of meat, and you'll each have a reasonable quantity. Or if there are no willing dining partners, order a half-sandwich with an extra slice of bread.

Submarine Shops—Best Choices

Let's consider the best choices in a sub shop. If you've got some calories to spare, go ahead and have the small-size sub roll. This will help fill you up and give you a good dose of carbos. If your calorie budget is tighter, have a Syrian pita pocket. They usually use about two-thirds of the pocket, which puts it in the range of 150 calories, probably half of what's in the small sub roll. The best meats to order are turkey, smoked turkey, roast beef, ham, and hot ham (this a great spicy choice). Use a limited amount of cheese, and only if you're not closely monitoring saturated fat and cholesterol intake.

Make sure to load up on fresh veggies. Ask that the preparer go light on the meats, hold the oil or mayonnaise, and load on the shredded lettuce, sliced tomatoes, onions, pickles, and hot peppers. The pickles and hot peppers will definitely add some sodium, but if that's not a big concern, have them piled on—they add great spicy flavor.

There are several salads to choose from as an alternative to the sub sandwich. These are commonly served with Italian bread or in a Syrian pita pocket. The usuals are tossed garden, chef salad, antipasto, Greek salad, and tossed salad offered with a scoop of tuna, chicken, or seafood. On some menus you'll find tossed or Greek salad served in a pita pocket. The tossed, chef (with some substitutes for lower-fat items if necessary), Greek, and tuna, chicken, or seafood salads, if you've got a few extra calories to spare, are fine choices. An antipasto, with all its high-fat and sodium ingredients, is best avoided. Remember, the biggest nutrition pitfall is the dressing.

Typical Menu: Luncheon Style

Soups	**New England clam chowder** (creamy chowder with minced clams and potatoes)
	✓ **Chili**
	✓ **Vegetable soup**
Salads	Served with choice of dressing: blue cheese, Thousand Island, Italian, French, ranch, ✓ lemon-garlic, or ✓ low-calorie Italian
✓ indicates preferred choices	✓ **House salad** (lettuce topped with peppers, mushrooms, cucumbers, and tomatoes)

✓ **Greek salad** (bed of lettuce topped with crumbled feta cheese, red onions, and Greek olives)

✓ **Chef salad** (bed of greens topped with ham, turkey, Swiss cheese, tomatoes, and cucumbers)

Tuna, chicken, or seafood salad (bed of greens with tomato, green peppers, and bean sprouts topped with a scoop of tuna, chicken, or seafood salad)

✓ **Roasted chicken salad** (roasted chicken sliced on bed of romaine lettuce, sliced tomato, and cucumber)

Cold Sandwiches*
✓ **Smoked turkey**
✓ **Roast beef**
Egg salad
Chicken salad
Tuna salad
Seafood salad
Hot pastrami
✓ **Corned beef**
✓ **Ham and cheese**
Club sandwich (choice of turkey or roast beef)

Hot Sandwiches*
Reuben (corned beef grilled with cheese and sauerkraut, topped with Thousand Island dressing)
✓ **Hamburgers**
Grilled cheese
✓ **Grilled chicken breast**
✓ **Bacon, lettuce, and tomato**
Grilled hot dog

Tuna melt (scoop of tuna salad with melted mozzarella cheese)

*All sandwiches are on choice of: ✓ submarine roll, white, ✓ whole-wheat, ✓ pumpernickel ✓ kaiser roll, croissant, or ✓ Syrian pocket.

Combinations	✓ **Soup and salad** (cup of any soup served with house or spinach salad) ✓ **Soup or salad and half-sandwich** (cup of any soup served with choice of cold sandwich)

Side Orders

French fries	Onion rings
✓ Taboöli salad	✓ Coleslaw
Potato salad	✓ Plain yogurt
Potato chips	✓ Popcorn
Corn chips	✓ Pretzels

Desserts

Chocolate-chip cookies
Chocolate cake
Apple pie
✓ Fresh fruit cup

May I Take Your Order

Low-Calorie Sample Meal

Roasted chicken salad (dressing on the side)
Quantity: 3 oz. meat; 2 cups salad
Exchanges: 3 meat (lean); 2 vegetable
Dressing (on the side)
Quantity: 2 tablespoons
Exchanges: 1 fat

Tabooli salad with lemon-herb
dressing
Quantity: ½ cup
Exchanges: 1 fat; 1 starch
Apple (brought from home)
Quantity: 1 small
Exchanges: 1 fruit
Mineral water
Quantity: 10 oz.
Exchanges: free

Nutrition Summary	425 calories
	21% calories as fat
	33% calories as protein
	46% calories as carbohydrate
	73 mg cholesterol
	862 mg sodium

Moderate-Calorie Sample Meal	**Vegetable soup**

Quantity: 1 cup
Grilled chicken breast sandwich
with lettuce, tomato and mustard
Quantity: 3 oz. meat
Syrian pocket for above
Quantity: ⅔ whole pocket
Fresh fruit cup
Quantity: ¾ cup
Milk, low-fat (skim preferable)
Quantity: 1 cup

Nutrition Summary	589 calories
	16% calories as fat
	31% calories as protein
	53% calories as carbohydrate
	73 mg cholesterol
	1437 mg sodium (800 accounted for by soup)

Healthier eating out
Salad Bar Style

"You guys go have your burgers and fries, it's the salad bar for me. I'm watching my waistline." How many times have you heard this virtuous statement echoed in the employee cafeteria, a local fast-food haven, or a steak house? Unfortunately, the well intended "healthy" trip, or trips, to an all-you-can-eat salad bar often results in a shockingly high-fat and high-calorie meal.

The word "salad" does bring to mind visions of lettuce, spinach, tomatoes, and peppers in a rainbow of colors. However, in and among these healthy salad bar "regulars" lurk the pasta salad, potato salad, marinated vegetables, pepperoni, cheeses, and other high-fat foods that boost calories way up. Lastly, and perhaps most damaging, the salad is topped off with dressing, often containing upward of 60 or 70 calories per tablespoon. So, under the guise of a "healthy" food choice, the salad bar, if not approached cautiously, can result in a very high-fat and high-calorie meal.

However, when approached with a plan in mind, more knowledge about wise and unwise food selections, and lots of self-discipline, the salad bar can be a nutritionally complete lunch or dinner.

THE MENU PROFILE

Before you even approach the salad bar, take a minute or two to do some preplanning. Think about how hungry you are. If hunger is about to get the better of you, remember, your eyes are bigger than your stomach. Rather than choosing with your eyes and taste buds, try to make decisions with your health goals in mind. Think about what foods you really want, and in what quantity. If you are unfamiliar with a particular salad bar, or items are constantly changing, take a moment to survey the entire bar.

As you begin making your choices, start with the raw vegetables. These are usually placed at the beginning of the salad bar. (See Table 1 at the end of this chapter, which delineates the best and the worst salad bar choices.)

The next ingredients to be layered on are the slightly higher calorie beets, chick peas, tuna, and others. You'll find several vegetables that are a bit higher in calories but by all means still very nutritious: carrots, beets, and onions are among these selections.

There are usually several items on the salad bar that help you add more carbohydrate without adding much fat—green peas, chick peas (also known as garbanzo beans), and kidney beans are among them. Chick peas and kidney beans might also be found in three-bean salad, which makes a frequent appearance at salad bars. For the most part, three bean is one of the better mixed salads to choose because it contains practically no fat.

For those wishing to add some relatively low-calorie protein foods to their salad, here are several choices: plain tuna (not mixed into tuna salad), ham, egg, feta cheese, and cottage cheese (likely, it will not be low fat). Two of these—ham and feta cheese—are high in sodium. Obviously, tuna, chicken, and seafood salad add protein, but they also add lots of fat. Cheese and pepperoni contain more calories from fat than from protein, and pepperoni especially adds sodium.

The bigger the salad bar, the more salad mixtures are available such as pasta salads, marinated vegetable salads, and others. Some of these are smart choices, and others should be left in the serving bowl. Generally speaking, marinated beets, marinated mixed vegetables or mushrooms, three-bean salad, a vinegar-based coleslaw, and mixed fruit salad are fine. Small quantities (about ¼ cup) should be taken, especially by those closely monitoring calories, sugar, and sodium intake.

Another place to pick up some hidden fat calories and possibly sodium is from the salad bar "accessories." There, temptations include nuts, seeds, Chinese dried noodles, olives, and bacon bits. These are usually added in small quantities, but observe their high-calorie contribution from the table that follows.

THE LOWDOWN ON SALAD DRESSINGS

By far the biggest culprit in adding abundant and hidden calories is the crowning touch—salad dressing. America's two favorite salad dressings are blue cheese and Thousand Island. These are among the highest fat and highest calorie dressings. Regular salad dressing, the type most frequently found at salad bars, rings in at about 60–80 calories per tablespoon. That's a level tablespoon, not heaping. In addition to the calories, the creamy dressings that contain mayonnaise, sour cream, and/or cheese have additional saturated fat not to be found in soy, cottonseed, or olive-oil-based salad dressings.

Salad dressings even though used in minimal quantity can contribute lots of sodium. Four tablespoons of either a regular or reduced-calorie dressing can provide in the range of 500 milligrams of sodium. Some of the no-oil dressings are even higher in sodium. Think about simply using oil and vinegar, which contains next to no sodium.

HEALTHY DRESSING STRATEGIES

By no means must you eat your salad without dressing. There are lots of healthy options. First, start by using less of your favorite dressing. Think about how much is usually left on the plate. Another option is to take half the amount of your favorite dressing and thin it with vinegar, lemon juice, or water. This cuts the calories (and also sodium) in half. From 400 to 200 is certainly a significant reduction. And believe it or not, using less dressing helps you enjoy the various tastes of the foods more.

These days it's common to find at least one reduced-calorie or "light" salad dressing. These dressings range from about 15–30 calories per tablespoon. That's half or less than half the calories of regular dressing. Another strategy is to purchase in the supermarket, especially for restaurant dining, individually packaged no-oil salad dressings.

If you have adequate self-discipline, a plan in mind, and some knowledge about what to select and what to avoid, a salad bar can be the health-conscious eater's paradise.

TABLE 1

Best to Worst Salad Bar Choices

Low-Calorie Vegetables (approx. 25 calories/1 cup)
broccoli
cabbage (red or green)
cauliflower
celery
cucumbers
endive
lettuce (all types)
peppers (all types)
radishes
sauerkraut*
spinach
sprouts (all types)
summer squash, raw
watercress
zucchini, raw

Higher-Calorie Vegetables (approx. 25 calories/½ cup)
artichoke, canned
beets, canned
carrots, raw
onions, raw (all types)
tomatoes, raw

Salad Bar "Accessories" (calories/tablespoon)	
pickles*	2–5
hot peppers	2–5
raisins	10
Chinese noodles	20
bacon bits (soy based)	27
sunflower seeds	47
olives, green or black*	50
peanuts	50
sesame seeds	52

Starches (60–100 calories/½ cup)
chick peas (garbanzo beans)
kidney beans
green peas
croutons (commercial)
crackers (4–6)
bread (1 slice or 1 oz.)
pita pocket (½)

Lean Protein (40–80 calories/oz.)
plain tuna
cottage cheese
egg
ham*
feta cheese*

Higher-Fat Protein (100+ calories/oz.)
cheeses*
pepperoni*

Salad Bar Mixtures (35–50 calories/¼ cup)
marinated/pickled beets
marinated artichoke hearts
three-bean salad
marinated assorted vegetables
marinated mushrooms
pasta salad, oil based
gelatin with fruit
fruit salad

Salad Bar Mixtures (50–80 calories/¼ cup)
tuna salad
chicken salad
seafood salad
corn relish
macaroni salad
potato salad
fruit ambrosia
pasta salad, mayonnaise-based

*Items particularly high in sodium.

16.

Healthier eating out
Breakfast and Brunch

Late for work, on vacation, on a business trip, it's Sunday morning, driving along the highway, or celebrating with a champagne brunch—just a few reasons why breakfast or brunch is eaten away from home. But in the main, breakfast is the meal most frequently eaten at home. Sadly, it is often skipped altogether.

A wise health and waist-watcher goal is to eat something for breakfast no matter what healthy foods you choose. A slice of last night's pizza, eaten cold, is better than a mid-morning bag of chips and can of regular soda. It doesn't have to be a traditional, hearty breakfast to be healthy. In fact, you're better off avoiding some traditional American breakfast foods as we'll see.

THE MENU PROFILE

Starters

The start to breakfast is often the automatic glass of orange juice. Few people are aware that even a six-ounce glass of almost any juice provides at least 60 calories. Don't get me wrong, those are healthy calories, but you'd be better off *eating* fruit rather than slurping it quickly. Try ordering a half-grapefruit, slice of melon, or fresh fruit instead of the usual glass of juice. Fruit will provide more fiber, more volume, and simply take you longer to eat. Fruit can also be used on cereal or on pancakes, French toast, or waffles in place of the high-calorie butter and syrup.

Cereals

Cold cereals are almost always available at breakfast restaurants. Often you've got several to choose from—Cornflakes, Puffed Wheat, Shredded Wheat, Rice Krispies, Raisin Bran, and Bran Flakes are among the regulars. It's best to use the whole-grain cereals; they provide more fiber. Almost all cold cereals, sugar coated or not, contain sugar or a form of sugar among the top four ingredients. People who have diabetes are told they can choose from any of the non-sugar-coated cereals. However, several have no sugar at all added, such as Shredded Wheat, Puffed Wheat, and Puffed Rice. Surprisingly, cold cereals have a chunk of sodium, on average about 250 milligrams.

Hot cereals are usually among the menu listings. Either oatmeal or cream of wheat are often available. Again, it's great to use the oat-based cereals to increase soluble fiber intake. Maybe we will soon see oat bran cereals appearing on menus. Hot cereals as well as cold cereals offer mainly carbohydrates and no fat (unless it is added).

Obviously, you're best off topping your cereal with low-fat or, better yet, skim milk. Low fat is about the best you can do in most restaurants. Avoid the whole milk and cream. Top cold or hot cereal with bananas or other fresh fruit.

Breakfast Entrees

Pancakes, French toast, and waffles are basically made from the same ingredients: flour, water, egg, a bit of sugar, and a leavening agent. Before the whipped butter and syrup are loaded on, they're really not nutritional disasters. Unfortunately, the portions are often way more than you need. To solve that problem, share an order or order a "short stack" of pancakes. If you ask the waitperson to hold the butter and you use only a bit of syrup, or top with fresh fruit, jam, jelly, or sugar substitute and cinnamon (especially good on French toast), their healthiness dramatically improves.

Eggs can be a big problem in restaurants because they usually come in duplicate or triplicate. Guidelines of the American Heart Association and other health organizations advise no more than 3–5 egg yolks per week. The largest problem with eggs is their cholesterol content, at 213 milligrams per egg. It all comes from the yolk. However, eggs are moderate in their saturated fat content. It's best to avoid the omelettes unless you're sharing a veggie one. If you're due for an egg, try ordering just one. Poaching requires no fat, whereas fat is used to scramble or fry an egg.

Breads

There are often numerous choices from the bread and bakery category—some smart and others better left on the baker's shelf. Let's start with the increasingly popular muffin. Unfortunately, muffins have received quite a bit of hype due to the emphasis on increasing fiber intake. On average, the 3–3½-ounce (on the large side) muffin contains in the range of 250–450 calories, about 30–35 percent of which come from fat. Surprisingly, the "healthier, high-fiber muffins" are not what they're cracked up to be. However, if you have a moderate-size bran or oat bran muffin without any added fats, then add a piece of fruit, that's a quick and reasonably healthy choice.

It's best to avoid the high-fat croissants, biscuits, Danish, doughnuts (especially deep-fried as opposed to cake type), and coffeecakes. Healthy breakfast breads, which contain ostensibly no fat, are toast, bagels, and English muffins. If you can choose whole-grain varieties, all the better.

The next step is to be careful about what you load on top. Request that any bread be served dry. Keep margarine, butter, cream cheese, and other fats to a minimum. Use the jams and jellies instead.

Side Dishes

The breakfast accompaniments can often add to the fat content. Think about the bacon, sausage, ham, or Canadian bacon that is served alongside eggs, pancakes, and French toast. They all add fat, sodium, and significant calories. The best of the choices, unless you are carefully monitoring sodium consumption, are ham and Canadian bacon because they are leaner. But it's best to avoid them all.

Breakfast potatoes, whether they are called hash browns or home fries, are another example of taking a great food—potatoes—and adding fat and sodium in the cooking process. The fast food varieties of breakfast potatoes derive at least 55 percent of their calories from fat. Ask how the potatoes are prepared. If they are homemade, they might be lighter in fat content than the pre-formed frozen and deep-fried potatoes.

Side orders appearing more frequently are yogurt and cottage cheese. Both can be healthy additions to any breakfast. Use these to top off fruit or breakfast breads. You might do best ordering *à la carte*, though it's not always economical. Try fresh fruit, yogurt, or cottage cheese and whole-wheat toast or a bagel. Or share an order of pancakes, French toast, or waffles and order yogurt and fresh fruit *à la carte* as a topping.

Typical Menu: Breakfast/Brunch Style

Fruits and Juices	✓ **Juices,** small or large (orange, grapefruit, apple, cranberry, tomato) ✓ **Grapefruit half** ✓ **Fresh fruit cup** ✓ **Sliced melon**
Cereals	✓ **Cold cereal** (cornflakes, Special K, Raisin Bran, bran flakes) **Granola** (natural, oat-based cereal filled with nuts and grains) ✓ **Hot cereal** (oatmeal, cream of wheat, cream of rice, Wheatena)
Pancakes, French Toast, Waffles	Served with whipped butter on top and syrup on the side ✓ **Buttermilk pancakes,** stack of 3, large ✓ **Silver dollar pancakes** (10–12 small buttermilk pancakes) ✓ **Blueberry pancakes** (3 large buttermilk pancakes filled with blueberries) **French toast** (4 halves of extra-thick bread, dipped in egg batter and grilled) ✓ **Belgian waffle**

✓ indicates
preferred
choices

Eggs	✓ **One egg** (fried, scrambled, or poached) **Two eggs** (fried, scrambled, or poached) **Eggs Benedict** (two English muffin halves, each topped with Canadian bacon, poached egg, and hollandaise sauce) **Steak and eggs** (2 eggs prepared to order and served with 8-oz. sirloin strip)
3-Egg Omelettes	**Western** (sauteed onions and green peppers; covered with cheddar cheese and diced ham) **Florentine** (spinach, onions, and feta cheese; topped with creamy mushroom sauce) ✓ **Veggie** (sauteed onions, green and red peppers, and mushrooms; topped with Swiss cheese)
Breads/Bakery	**Croissant** ✓ **Muffin** (choice of blueberry, raisin bran, or oat bran) ✓ **Bagel** with low-fat cream cheese **Danish pastry** (choice of apple or cheese) **Doughnut** **Biscuit** ✓ **Toast** (choice of white, whole-wheat, rye, or pumpernickel) ✓ **English muffin**
Side Orders	**Bacon** **Sausage,** links or patties ✓ **Ham** **Home fries** **Hash browns** **Cottage cheese**

✓ **Fruited or plain yogurt**
✓ **Fresh fruit**

May I Take Your Order

Low-Calorie Sample Meal	**Banana,** sliced *Quantity:* ½ *Exchanges:* 1 fruit **Cold or hot cereal** (high-fiber, bran, oatmeal, or oat bran) *Quantity:* 1 box or 1 cup *Exchanges:* 1½ starch **Milk, low-fat** (skim preferable) *Quantity:* 1 cup *Exchanges:* 1 milk
Nutrition Summary	272 calories 13% calories as fat 16% calories as protein 71% calories as carbohydrate 18 mg cholesterol 342 mg sodium
Moderate-Calorie Sample Meal	**Orange juice** *Quantity:* 6 oz. *Exchanges:* 1½ fruit **Egg, poached** *Quantity:* 1 *Exchanges:* 1 meat (med.) **Bagel** (cream cheese on the side) *Quantity:* 1 small *Exchanges:* 2 starch **Veggie cream cheese** for above *Quantity:* 1 tablespoon *Exchanges:* 1 fat **Home fries** *Quantity:* ½ cup *Exchanges:* 1 fat; 1 starch

Nutrition Summary	541 calories
	37% calories as fat
	12% calories as protein
	51% calories as carbohydrate
	228 mg cholesterol
	560 mg sodium

Moderate-Calorie Sample Meal

Orange juice
Quantity: 6 oz.
French toast (hold the butter)
Quantity: 1 order
Maple syrup for above
Quantity: 2 tablespoons
Milk, low-fat (skim preferable)
Quantity: 1 cup

Nutrition Summary	574 calories
	22% calories as fat
	13% calories as protein
	65% calories as carbohydrate
	135 mg cholesterol
	640 mg sodium

17.

Healthier eating out
Airline Style

The often-maligned average airline meal has improved noticeably in recent years. But let's face it, providing food service to many people at minimal cost in a crowded plane without the conveniences of a well-equipped restaurant is a difficult task at best.

From peanuts, the expected handout with your beverage, to creamy salad dressings and thick gravies, airline foods are often laden with fat and salt. A redeeming factor is that the portions are quite small, so even if you eat a high percentage of calories as fat, you're not eating that many calories.

The airlines do get credit for becoming more responsive to the health demands of flyers. With more and more people flying, either for business or pleasure, there are more demands for healthier foods.

In actuality people have been ordering special-diet meals on planes for years. Low calorie, low cholesterol, low sodium, diabetic, and other special meals have been available for quite a while. More recently, many airlines have improved the healthiness of their standard fare—from less salty snack foods to more chicken and fish and less gooey desserts.

Probably the best kept secret about airline food is that anyone can order a special meal on most of the major domestic carriers—from vegetarian to low cholesterol and children's plates. No one needs a medical or religious reason for ordering any one of the special meals. And there is no additional charge. All you need is a phone and a voice.

SPECIAL MEALS FOR ALL

There's an amazing array of special meals available. Some of the special-diet offerings are diabetic, low calorie (though they don't state the number of calories), low cholesterol, low sodium, and bland. For people who avoid certain foods due to personal preference or for religious reasons, there are vegetarian meals, kosher, and several airlines even provide Hindu, oriental, and Muslim meals. For the young traveler, infants', toddlers', and children's meals are available from certain airlines when ordered in advance.

Possibly the best choice on airlines is the fruit or seafood plate. These are often better choices because they're served cold. There is less taste and palatability damage done to cold food than hot when it's held for a long time. Even if you're on a low cholesterol, fat, or sodium meal plan, the fruit or seafood might be a better choice than the special meal. It most likely will fit into your guidelines and taste better as well.

The fruit plate can range from simply an array of fresh fruit to fruit with cottage cheese and/or yogurt and crackers. The seafood plate might be shrimp or seafood salad, served with greens, dressing, and crackers. These are very nice light alternatives. Watch out, though—you'll have the other

passengers staring at your tray with desiring eyes.
They might angrily ask how you managed to get that.
Be nice and take a minute to give them some healthy
advice.

HOW TO ORDER MEALS

It's surprisingly simple to have a special meal waiting with your name on it as your plane taxis down
the runway. Most of the airlines specify that you provide at least 24-hours notice for special meals. It's
easiest to order the special meals when you make
reservations. For frequent flyers who consistently
use the same travel agent, just specify the meal you
want when you make your call. They will list it in
your record as they do seat preferences.

BEVERAGES AND SNACKS

Most flyers know that they will at least be served a
beverage. The free choices are generally consistent
from airline to airline—coffee, tea, carbonated beverages, mineral waters, and juices. If you are choosing a hot beverage and want to add cream, be careful
of the definition of cream. They might have the non-
dairy powders or liquid whiteners that often contain
coconut oil. A bit of whole or low-fat (preferable)
milk is a better and often an available choice. Alternative sweeteners are always on board.

   As for cold beverages, if you're carefully monitoring calories, you're best off with the low-calorie
carbonated ones, club soda, or mineral waters—all
of which usually are in large supply. Tomato juice or
my favorite, Bloody Mary mix (hold the vodka), are
also low-calorie choices. Juices are alternatives, but
don't forget a 12-ounce can of juice can run up to
almost 200 calories.

   On many flights a small bag of peanuts, salted
or honey-coated, will be placed on your tray with
your beverage. These delicious little nuggets are a bit
of protein loaded with fat. You're better off purchas-
ing a small bag of pretzels or popcorn prior to board-

ing the plane, or just say "no thanks" to the bag of peanuts.

On flights of one to two hours but not within particular meal times, you might be served a snack. Some times the snacks are more palatable than the hot meal. Again, it's likely due to the fact that these foods are not cooked, frozen, and then reheated prior to serving. Snacks usually include a small sandwich with meat and cheese or crackers and cheese. Fruit, chocolates, or cookies are also often included. Some airlines do have special diet snacks. To find out, simply ask when you're making reservations.

18.

Healthier drinking out

Beverages

In many dining situations the first question you are asked is, "May I bring you something to drink?" In some restaurants the choices may simply be soda, coffee, or water. However, often the whole gamut of beverages from water to distilled spirits to brandy or liqueur is offered before, during, and after the meal. Since beverages are an integral part of eating out and because lots of calories, unhealthy ones, can be contributed, you need to have a plan and a response to the question, "May I bring you something to drink?"

Health Considerations

There certainly are medical and health factors to consider when making the decision to select an alcoholic beverage. From a general good health and nutrition perspective, moderation is the magic word when it comes to alcohol consumption. Heavy imbibing is correlated with many diseases. It is also well known that you'd be hard pressed to find much nutritional value in alcohol. In fact, excessive alcohol intake, in lieu of adequate food consumption, is known to result in nutrient deficiencies.

The positive, healthy aspects of moderate alcohol consumption have been connected with stress reduction and modestly raising HDLs—the "good" cholesterol (high density lipoproteins). However, with all aspects considered, most health professionals would not make the recommendation to start drinking or to increase alcohol consumption just to derive those benefits. That holds true especially in light of the minimal nutritional benefits and excess calories found in alcoholic drinks.

People attempting to lose weight or maintain their newly found waistlines should practice strict moderation when it comes to alcohol. You simply can't afford the calories.

Beer

It might be labeled Singha in Thai restaurants, Tsing Tsao in Chinese restaurants, Dos Equis in Mexican eating spots, and Bud or Mich when eating American style. But basically beer is beer, whether it is from Thailand or brewed here in the U.S. Beer is a brewed and fermented drink. Its taste is created from blending malted barley and other starches and flavoring the brew with hops. Interestingly, *sake,* a Japanese drink, is a refermented brewed beverage made from rice.

There are very few differences nutritionally and calorically from one beer to the next. Bottom line—the calories add up fast. A 12-oz. can of regular beer contains about 150 calories. And how many people drink just one? With beer, there certainly is an alternative: light beer. Most light beers ring in at about 100 calories for 12 oz. Obviously, that can add up quickly, too, but it might be a helpful alternative when trying to minimize calories.

Wine

Whether it's red, white, or rosé, domestic or imported, wine contains about 120 calories for 6 ounces. So, if you really like red wine better than white or fruity wine better than dry, the best advice is to drink less but drink what you enjoy. If you are used to splitting a bottle of wine, you might want to reduce the quantity you consume by simply ordering a half-carafe or ordering by the glass. Today, many restaurants offer a selection of better wines by the glass rather than simply the house red or white, which are often unexciting.

A few suggestions. Always make sure you have a non-caloric beverage by your side along with the glass of wine. That way, you can use the non-caloric beverage to quench your thirst and you are more likely to sip the wine, making it last longer. If you wish to limit yourself to one glass of wine and you really enjoy it with your meal, don't order it until the meal arrives. Order a non-caloric beverage to accompany your dining companions as they sip their alcoholic drinks.

Another calorie-conscious strategy is to order a wine spritzer, again white, red, or rosé doesn't matter. A wine spritzer is made with wine, club soda, and a twist of lemon or lime. What's nice about a spritzer is that you get a nice, tall, thirst-quenching drink with a small amount of wine and thus limited calories. So, for the same number of calories in one glass of wine, you can have two wine spritzers.

Try to avoid spritzers made with sweetened soda, wine punches with juices, or wine coolers; the "mixes" in all of these add calories. It is common to find sangria by the pitcher in Mexican restaurants. Sangria is best avoided due to the extra calories from additional ingredients such as fruit juices and granulated sugar.

Champagne is actually classified as wine. It is most often used as a celebratory beverage or to toast an occasion. Small quantities are usually consumed. Champagne is slightly higher in calories than most wines, and the calories are somewhat dependent on how dry it is. Drier champagne is slightly higher in calories.

Distilled Spirits

Rum, gin, vodka, and whiskey are all classified as distilled spirits. Interestingly, like wine, they all have the same number of calories—about 100 per jigger (1½ oz.) for 80-proof liquor. Many people have the misconception that rum, scotch, and bourbon are higher in calories than gin and vodka. That misconception might relate to the fact that these distilled spirits are often found in sweeter drinks or taste slightly sweeter and more concentrated than vodka and gin. Actually, 100 calories per shot is not bad when compared to the calories of other alcoholic beverages. So if hard liquor is what you prefer, don't get caught up in the misconception that wine and beer have less calories. But certainly you get more volume for your calories with wine and beer.

The bigger problem with distilled spirits is that they are often mixed with other high-calorie ingredients. Consider a tequila sunrise made with tequila, orange juice, and grenadine (a sweet, red syrup), or a rusty nail made with Drambuie and scotch. These drinks are closer to the 150–200 calorie range. It's best to avoid drinks that are a combination of distilled spirits and another liquor, cordial, fruit juices, sugar, sweetened soda, tonic water, or cream. Think about ordering a vodka, rum, gin, or whiskey on the rocks, with a splash of water, club soda, or diet soda. Diet tonic water is also produced but not often stocked in restaurant bars.

Liqueur and Brandy

The last category of alcoholic beverages is liqueurs, cordials, and brandies. Liqueurs and cordials synonymously describe beverages such as the familiar Kahlua, Amaretto, and Drambuie. These drinks are most commonly used straight as an after-dinner drink or in combination with other distilled spirits in a mixed drink. Brandy is created from distilled wine or the mash of fruit. The most familiar brandy is cognac, but other popular examples are Greek Metaxa and kirsch (a cherry brandy).

Liqueurs, cordials, and brandies ring in at about 150 calories per jigger (1½ oz.), a substantial number of calories for a small quantity. They are often consumed in addition to other alcoholic beverages, following a meal. However, if you decide that is what you want and you have "budgeted" the calories, then sip away slowly.